CITYSPOTS
RIGA

Ann Carroll Burgess, Tom Burgess

Written by Ann Carroll Burgess & Tom Burgess
Original photography by Ann Carroll Burgess & Tom Burgess
Front cover photography courtesy of Alamy Images

Produced by 183 Books
Design/layout/maps: Chris Lane and Lee Biggadike
Editorial/project management: Stephen York

Published by Thomas Cook Publishing
A division of Thomas Cook Tour Operations Limited
PO Box 227, Units 15/16, Coningsby Road
Peterborough PE3 8SB, United Kingdom
email: books@thomascook.com
www.thomascookpublishing.com
+44 (0)1733 416477

First edition © 2006 Thomas Cook Publishing
Text © 2006 Thomas Cook Publishing
Maps © 2006 Thomas Cook Publishing
ISBN-13: 978-1-84157-553-7
ISBN-10: 1-84157-553-4
Head of Thomas Cook Publishing: Chris Young
Project Editor: Kelly Anne Pipes
Production/DTP: Steven Collins

Printed and bound in Spain by GraphyCems

CONTENTS

SYMBOLS & ABBREVIATIONS

The following symbols are used throughout this book:

☎ telephone **✆** fax **ⓔ** email **ⓦ** website address
ⓐ address **🕒** opening times **ⓝ** public transport connections

The following symbols are used on the maps:
ℹ Tourist Information Office
✈ Airport

Hotels and restaurants are graded by approximate price as follows:
£ budget price **££** mid-range price **£££** expensive
The local currency is the Lat (see page 141)

Latvian words in addresses:
iela street
bulvaris (bulv.) boulevard
laukums square

24-HOUR CLOCK

All times in this book are given in the 24-hour clock system used widely in Europe and in most international transport timetables.

◑ *Riga's Old Town is dominated by spires*

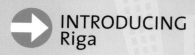

Introduction

Riga engages in a delicate balancing act. One foot is firmly planted in the Soviet-influenced 20th century, while the other stands on tiptoe in the new millennium.

With a population greater than 740,000, Riga is not just Latvia's but the Baltic States' largest city. It bustles with urban energy, as it should: commerce lies at the very heart of the city. Once a member of the Hanseatic League, Riga owes its financial development and stature in the Baltics to trade.

It was trade and commerce that gave this city the architecture that enchants so many visitors. Riga is a treasure chest of design, from the sumptuousness of Nordic Gothic, Classic Symbolism, art nouveau and Constructivism, to the utilitarian influences of Soviet occupation.

Riga's varied collection of architecture is so important that the historic centre of Riga, the Old Town, was added to the UNESCO World Heritage List in 1997.

Contributing to Riga's unusual nature is the ethnic split of the city. More than half of the city's residents are Russian or Russian-speaking, the remaining population Latvian. The result is two communities appearing to lead separate lives, reading different newspapers, and listening to radio and television stations broadcast in their own language. Fortunately for the visitor, English and German are widely spoken.

Where the people of Riga join hands is in the celebration of holidays. The summer solstice brings all of Riga to its feet and into the countryside to celebrate the longest day of the year. There are numerous festivals throughout the year, sparking occasions for more drinking and celebrating. And, since Christian roots run deep in this country, Christmas is also important. In fact, Riga is credited with the first decorated Christmas tree.

Like a patchwork quilt of the centuries, Riga is a little bit this and a little bit that. Some will tell you it has the cosy intimacy of Prague, the sophistication of Paris or the cosmopolitan flavour of Berlin. Riga has all that and more. It has its own personality, born of hardship, conquest and endurance. As always, Riga will emerge stronger than ever, having simply added one more layer to its soul, one more set of treasures for visitors to discover.

⬤ *The cathedral square is taken over by the Christmas Market in December*

When to go

SEASONS & CLIMATE

Misty. Ethereal. Moody. Atmospheric. Whatever you want to call the weather in Riga, it is almost invariably drizzly and cloudy. Riga's climate is controlled by incoming streams from the Atlantic Ocean, moderated by the Baltic Sea. This gives Riga a very moderate, maritime climate, with summers not too hot, and winters not too cold. The humidity in summer can be high, up to 80 per cent. Thus, Riga tends to be rather cloudy and damp, with over 700 mm (28 in) of precipitation a year on average. Summer temperatures average 17°C (62°F) and rarely exceed 22°C (72°F).

Spring starts in mid-April, and comes in quickly, with an explosion of green in the fields, and multicoloured flowers everywhere. May, the first half of June, August and September are the best months to visit. Thunder showers are frequent during the last half of June. July, although the warmest month, is also the wettest, with frequent showers. March is the driest month.

Winter gets serious in November and lasts until March, with snow usually on the ground from mid-December until mid-March. Winter temperatures average -5°C (23°F) and rarely go over 4°C (39°F). Spring and autumn tend to be unpredictable, commonly with both sunshine and rain on the same day.

ANNUAL EVENTS

Most major holidays and traditions in Latvian culture can trace their roots to sun-worshipping pagan cultures. The most important holiday on the Latvian calendar is **Jani**, or the Summer Solstice, celebrated on the nights of 23 and 24 June. This is when the city is emptied of people, as they head to the countryside to enjoy the

ALL SINGING, ALL DANCING

The Quadrennial Song and Dance Festival has been celebrated since it was first held, in 1873. From June to the end of August over 30,000 singers and 15,000 dancers from all the Baltic States, dressed in national costume, gather in Riga for a summer festival of folk life, held at various venues and culminating in a parade through the city to the grand open-air stage in Mezaparks. This festival always seems to strengthen the spiritual bonds and self-esteem of Latvians. As its name implies, it rolls round every 4 years, the next being in 2008.

shortest night of the year, spent in the company of friends, singing songs, dancing and drinking beer.

Christmas has always been a special event in Latvia, pre-dating Christianity back to the pagan festivities to celebrate the returning of the sun after the shortest day. In 1510 the world's first decorated Christmas tree was erected in Riga. Today, Riga's Christmas Market is one of the best in Europe, with plenty of crafts, handiwork, sugary treats and night-time holiday spirit.

February
International Bach Chamber Music Festival Concerts of Bach's chamber music pieces are held in buildings entirely appropriate to the music, as well as in larger concert halls and even the House of the Blackheads (see pages 65–67). The festival also features master classes by famous musicians.

March
Baltic Ballet Festival Created in 1993, the Ballet Festival brings together ballet soloists, companies and choreographers from all three Baltic states. ⓦ www.ballet-festival.lv

May
Riga International Marathon Annual event that draws runners from around the globe. ⓦ www.marathon.lv

June
Gadatirgus A large arts and crafts festival held in the Old Town and various other venues.
Jani The annual midsummer pagan celebration. There's no better time to drink beer and celebrate the long summer days.
Opera Festival, Riga The Opera Festival is new to the Baltic scene but has high hopes of being included among the world's best opera festivals. Over a period of 10 days, two operas will be presented, including five performances by the Latvia National Opera.
ⓦ www.music.lv/opera

July
Early Music Festival Various venues in Riga, Bauska & Rundale.
ⓦ www.concerts.lv
Sigulda Opera Festival, Sigulda The music of Strauss, Bizet, Puccini or Wagner, depending upon the theme, with international artists performing at the Gala Concert. ⓦ www.sigulda.lv

August
Liepajas Dzintars A rock music festival held in Liepaja in mid-August.
Sacred Music Festival, Riga Choirs, composers and artists, both local

and guest, celebrate the music of composers such as Bach, Berlioz, Beethoven, Garuta and Vasks. Ⓦ www.music.lv/choirs/SMF

September
International Chamber Choir Festival, Riga
Ⓦ www.culture.lv/choirfestival
International Organ Music Festival, Liepaja Original organ compositions, choirs and guest artists highlight this festival held in Liepaja's famous Church of the Holy Trinity. Ⓦ www.liepaja.lv

October
International Chamber Music Festival, Riga Ⓦ www.arenafest.lv

December & January
Christmas Market Riga's Christmas Market began once again in 2001 after years of Soviet suppression. The emphasis is on hand crafts and performers in a festive atmosphere held in Doma laukums 1–31 December.
New Year In Riga A street party held in and around the Old Town's main square. Wrap up and greet the New Year in Latvian style!

PUBLIC HOLIDAYS
New Year's Day 1 Jan
Easter – Good Friday, Easter Sunday, Easter Monday Mar–Apr
Labour Day 1 May
Summer solstice celebrations (Ligo & Jani) 23–24 June
Proclamation Day of the Republic of Latvia 18 Nov
Christmas 24–26 Dec
New Year's Eve 31 Dec

Winter sports in Latvia

Latvia is a northern country with long winters, so it is no surprise that winter sports dominate the sport scene in Riga.

ICE HOCKEY

Currently, ice hockey is number one, and many consider it the national sport of Latvia. In 2000, the underdog Latvian team defeated the mighty Russians in the early matches of the World Championships, and thrust Latvia into the world hockey spotlight. Ever since, the Latvian team has continued to be placed in the top ten in the World Championships. Many of the top Latvian players are now in the National Hockey League. Riga invested over €30 million to build a new world-class arena to host the 2006 World Ice Hockey Championships, the largest sports event in the history of Latvia.

International Ice Hockey Arena ⓐ Skanstes iela 21, about 2 km (1.5 miles) north-east of the city centre.

BOBSLEIGH

Latvians are world-class bobsleighers, and you can try their sport. The run is in Sigulda, about 60 km (37 miles) east of Riga (see pages 115–116), and the track is just a few hundred metres west of the train station. It is open to the public winter and summer, Sat and Sun 12.00–17.00, at a cost of L3 per person. They will not let you go down nearly as fast as the Olympic team does, at, some 125 km/h.

▶ *The Latvians are aiming to be top dogs in the ice hockey world*

History

By European standards, Riga is quite young, only about 800 years. But its short history is one of occupation and endurance. Local tribes had inhabited the area for many years. The first foreign occupation started late in the 12th century when German crusaders and merchants took over the area. They officially founded Riga in 1201 by building a fortification. In 1211 the foundations for the Dome Cathedral were laid. Riga became a German military centre for the Baltic. In 1282, the town joined the Hanseatic League and grew economically from trade.

As a result of the Livonian War, Riga fell under the rule of Poland in 1558, but obtained status as a free town in 1561. Then Poland waged war with Sweden and in 1621 Riga fell to the Swedes, and became a Swedish administrative centre.

Sweden, in turn, lost Riga to the Russian Empire in 1710 in the aftermath of the so-called Northern War. In 1812, Riga was attacked by Napoleon's army, and the suburbs were burned. After this, the current street plan was created.

Under Tsarist Russia, Riga thrived. Industry rapidly grew, and the city became one of the main seaports of the Russian Empire. It grew in size until it was second only to St Petersburg in western Russia.

World War I was devastating to Riga. At the outbreak of war, Riga was in the front line, and about 200,000 inhabitants, along with industrial enterprises, were evacuated to Central Russia.

On 18 November 1918, with the collapse of Germany and with Russia weak from revolution, Latvia proclaimed independence. However, it took another two years of prolonged fighting to establish independence. In August 1920 a peace treaty with Russia was signed, and Riga become the capital of a free Latvia.

Riga flourished as part of independent Latvia. Once again it became a robust seaport, with development of industries, as well as culture and education. It was during this period that most of the art nouveau architecture (*Jugendstil*) was built.

Independence lasted only 20 years, until World War II. On 17 June 1940 Russian tanks rolled onto the streets of Riga. The following year the Germans threw the Russians out of the city. Two years later, the Russians were back. Riga suffered greatly in the war, with her ports and railway junctions totally destroyed.

Riga was an important part of Soviet Russia during the Cold War, mainly as a military base. Extensive immigration from other parts of the Soviet Union occurred, and today a very large portion of the city's population is Russian.

With the collapse of Soviet Russia, Latvia once again strove to become independent. A declaration to restore independence was adopted on 4 May 1990. In January 1991 the population of Latvia gathered on barricades to face down the Russian military. Finally, on 21 August 1991, Latvia, with Riga as its capital, once more declared independence. Since then Riga has spent considerable time and effort to restore the city to its former grandeur. On 1 May 2004 Latvia joined the European Union, promising a new era which will bring this northern capital back to the forefront of the European stage.

● *The flag of independent Latvia*

Lifestyle

Which Riga will you visit? The traditional city, with its Old Town medieval architecture, folk singing and hearty food, or the new Riga of gaudily decorated transmission towers, techno and hip-hop bars, Finnish cell phones and internet cafés?

It has been little more than a decade since Latvia regained its independence, and like a child let loose in a sweetshop, Latvians are gorging on all those things they had been denied, most importantly all the trappings of the decadent Western lifestyle.

In almost no time at all strip malls, valet parking and McDonald's have sprung up like weeds in an historical garden. But, hey, what's wrong with wanting a shopping centre? We might find it charming that a small town only has a bakery, but to the residents who must travel elsewhere to find groceries it's a nuisance.

The most developed part of Riga is the Old Town with its newer restaurants, upgraded hotels and cutting-edge music scene. By contrast the centre of the city and the suburban areas are most in need of improvement.

If you are heading to Riga on business, be prepared to dress in a fairly conservative style to meetings. Handshakes remain *de rigeur* for introductions and gifts are always appreciated. A good single malt will not go unnoticed. The country is still struggling with its transition from the communist state to a market economy and has some very serious problems to solve. But for the average resident in Riga life is not so different from any other industrialised nation. People queue for a driver's licence and at check-out counters in grocery stores. Sometimes the elevators don't work and the transit system is not as modern or clean as it could be. But you can always blame the malfunction on Soviet influences.

The darker side to Riga, and Latvia in general, is the almost apartheid-like attitude toward Russian-speaking residents. When the country regained its independence in 1991 it instituted a law granting citizenship only to those who had been Latvian citizens before 1940 and to their descendants. Today, some 500,000 (out of a population of 2.3 million) hold no passport at all. They are not citizens of Latvia, or anywhere else. These are residents who are prevented from voting, holding public office or working in the public sector. Be sure to brush up on a few phrases of Latvian as the Russian language is not well received by native Latvians.

During the Middle Ages Riga was a centre of commerce and little has changed since those days. Today the city is still the hub of trade and finance for the country. This new capitalism may be what launches Riga into the new millennium, complete with shopping malls and plugged-in citizens.

Young Latvians have taken readily to Western culture

Culture

Latvia has a rich and textured cultural life that includes music, theatre, festivals, films, museums and art galleries. The city is a true hub of culture in the Baltic area and hardly a day will pass without a renowned musician or performer making an appearance in Riga. More importantly, since the end of the Soviet occupation in 1991, there has been a renaissance movement to restore Latvian culture.

Folk life, folk arts and folk music are an integral part of Latvian culture. This is a country that doesn't simply celebrate its traditions, it elevates them to a pinnacle in every citizen's heart. The Latvian Quadennial Song and Dance Festival has drawn thousands of performers, and even more spectators, to a summer-long fest of traditional music, art and costume (see page 9).

Opera is important to this city, and most of the soloists and members of the chorus of the Latvian National Opera were trained first at the Latvian Academy of Music and then continued their studies abroad before returning home. The Opera House has been reopened and interest in performances is running high.

Latvia, and Riga in particular, has been hailed as a bastion of ballet excellence. While under the domain of the Soviets, Riga was ranked third in importance as a ballet centre, after the Kirov and the Bolshoi. Over the years the Riga Ballet, officially known as the Ballet Company of the Latvian National Opera, has gained world renown through the performances of such stars as Mikhail Barishnikov, Aleksandr Godunov and Maris Liepa. The company performs both classical and modern works of choreography.

No less important are the theatre arts in Latvia. Theatre in Riga

---

● *Look upwards for striking art nouveau details on the city's buildings*

Folk festivals are a much-loved expression of national pride

can trace its roots as far back as the 13th century. In the 1970s Riga was regarded as the hub of avant-garde productions, and traces of that spirit can be seen decades later.

Film making has grown over the last few decades, mostly with documentary movies, many of which have won awards internationally. Latvians are devout movie-goers and you'll find no shortage of newly released films in the capital's theatres.

And the museums. Ah, the museums. With more than 50 within the city of Riga it justifiably earns the title of the 'City of Museums'. History, the wars, maritime life, arts, decorative arts, medicine, writing, theatre, music, automobiles, telephones and railways all have their very own museum. Didn't find what you want on that list? There are also museums devoted to sport, photography, television, dolls, architecture and electricity. It is within these museums, particularly the smaller and more specialised, that you will find Latvia through the eyes of the artists, inventors and citizens who have lived in this fascinating city.

Despite wartime destruction, Riga remains an architectural delight

MAKING THE MOST OF
Riga

Shopping

BEST BUYS

Let's cut to the chase. The first thing to buy is Laima chocolate, which can only be described as divinely decadent. Then try on some pieces of Baltic amber at any of the souvenir or antique shops in the Old Town. Wrap yourself in a fashionable piece of Latvian linen, incredibly cheap compared to European prices. Then follow your purchases with a shot of the national drink, black balsam, a liqueur made from herbs, flowers and medicinal roots. An acquired taste, you can find it in most food stores and spirit shops. And there you have it, the complete Baltic food, drink and shopping experience.

WHERE TO SHOP

Shopping in Riga can be really expensive. For reasons unknown, this city's consumer goods are inexplicably more highly priced than anywhere else in the Baltic. However, if you must shop until you drop you'll find most of the best shops concentrated around the Old Town area and near the city centre. Malls are beginning to invade the Latvian shopping scene, but so far the results could only improve.

However, you could spend your time waiting for a train to the countryside by shopping at Origo, a shopping centre that straddles the newly renovated Central Station. Who would have imagined you could turn such a dull, but functional, space into a lively place? You can buy and do almost anything you might need here – get a computer part, drop off your dry cleaning, grab some flowers for

● *Although supermarkets are making inroads, traditional produce markets are still where most Latvians buy their food*

your main squeeze and stop for a cocktail. There are hundreds of shops, cafés and services within this location.

Near Central Station you'll find Central Market, housed in five enormous World War I-era Zeppelin hangars; It is a bustling, noisy and smelly place that you should not miss. If they make it or grow it you're sure to find someone selling it here. This is a perfect place to pick up the makings of an impromptu picnic. You can also find fake designer watches and Russian fur hats, but don't expect to find anything of real quality.

Can't live without a day spent crawling the mall? Each section of the city from the Old Town to the suburbs now has its own share of shopping malls. Centrs, once Soviet-owned, is now in the hands of a Norwegian firm that successfully transformed the department store into a Western-style mall with speciality shops, fast foods and a grocery store, Rimi, downstairs.

● *Riga excels in handmade toys and gift items*

Stockmann's, the venerable Finnish department store, has finally arrived in Riga. Four floors of fashion will keep even the most devoted shopaholic happy for a few hours. The delicatessen also offers up some goodies for a picnic in the park or for midnight munchies in your hotel room.

USEFUL SHOPPING PHRASES

What time do the shops open/close?
Cikos veikali tiek atvērti/slēgti?
Cikos veikali tiek atvehrti/slegti?

How much is this?
Cik tas maksā?
Tsik tas maksa?

Can I try this on?
Vai drīkstu to uzmērīt?
Vai drikstu to uzmehreet?

Can you show me the one in the window/this one?
Vai variet man parādīt to, kas ir logā/šo?
Vai variet man paradit to, kas ir loga/sho?

My size is...
Mans izmērs ir....
Mans izmers ir....

I'll take this one, thank you
Šo lūdzu, paldies
Sho ludzu, paldies

Do you have anything cheaper/larger/smaller/of better quality?
Vai jums ir kaut kas lētāks/lielāks/mazāks/labākas kvalitātes?
Vai yums ir kaut kas letaks/lielaks/ mazaks/labakas kvalitates?

Eating & drinking

Latvian cuisine is an adventure in cholesterol. Traditionally, Latvians are farmers who raise cows and other animals, so their diet is rich in meat and dairy products, with pork, cheese and sour cream involved in some manner with almost every dish. Bread holds a place of honour on the Latvian table, as it symbolises wealth.

Meals were an important part of daily life on the farms, with whole families gathering around large tables for the evening meal, discussing the events of the day and enjoying unhurried meals based on the fruits of their labour.

Today in Riga, starters and snacks include: *rasols*, a salad of diced meat, herring, potatoes, peas, carrots and pickles, all glued together with sour cream and mayonnaise; *piragi*, dough stuffed with cabbage and/or bacon bits; *pelmeni*, a Latvian version of ravioli; savoury pancakes filled with cheese or ham; potato pancakes; pork in aspic; smoked sausage; herring; smoked eel; and cabbage soup.

The local favourites to have with a round of beer are *pelekie zerni*, mushy green peas cooked in smoky bacon fat, and *zirnu pikas*, peas and bacon bits mashed and moulded into balls.

For the main course, the top of the local menu has specialities such as *karbonade*, a chop or lightly breaded schnitzel, and *fileja*, a fillet of pork, beef or chicken. Cuts of pork and other meats traditionally come with a nice rind of fat around the edge, since serving lean meat is considered rude. Main dishes based on salmon and trout are now becoming more common and main courses usually come with boiled potatoes or French fries, coleslaw, and pickled vegetables. Garnishes include sour cream and mushroom sauce. Meals are normally served with white bread and dark rye bread.

A favourite Latvian dessert is *kiselis*, an oat-porridge sweetened with seasonal fruit and berries. Other desserts include ice cream, tortes and cakes.

If the traditional Latvian food is too heavy for you, do not despair.

USEFUL DINING PHRASES

I would like a table for ... people
Es vēlos galdu ... cilvēkiem
Es velos galdu ... cilvekiem

Could I have it well-cooked/medium/rare please?
Man, lūdzu, labi izceptu/vidēji/izceptu?
Man, loodzu, labi iztseptu/videyi/iztseptu?

I am a vegetarian. Does this contain meat?
Es esmu veģetārietis. Vai tajā ir gaļa?
Es esmu vedyetahrietis. Vai tayah ir galya?

Where is the toilet (restroom) please?
Kur ir tualete?
Kur ir tualete?

I would like a beer/two beers, please
Es vēlos alu/divus alus, lūdzu
Es velos alu/divas alus, ludzu

Waiter! Waitress!
Oficiant! Oficiante!
Ofitsant! Ofitsante!

May I have the bill please?
Lūdzu rēķinu!
Ludzu rekyinu!

Chicken, fish and salads are beginning to invade the menus of many establishments, providing leaner choices for those who do not want to pack on the pounds.

As Riga becomes more cosmopolitan, a much wider variety of ethnic foods from around the world is becoming available.

On the liquid side, the Latvians prefer coffee during the day, and beer in the evening. Rigans frequent coffee shops in the daytime, and they normally take it black. If you want cream or sugar, you will have to ask for it. Beer normally comes as a regular lager, or as a dark porter, and the locals consume a lot of both. The traditional Latvian spirit is *Rigas melnais balsams* or Riga black balsam. The recipe is 250 years old, and combines roots, grasses and herbs. It is rather bitter, and is easier to take watered down with cola or some other mixer. Thanks to the Russian influence, good, cheap vodka is also readily available.

Restorans, meaning restaurant, indicates a more upmarket and expensive establishment, complete with starched white tablecloths and starched waiting staff. There are many of these in Riga, including in most major hotels. For something more informal, try a *krog* or *krodzins*, which is pub-like, often with rustic furnishings. At the bottom of the food chain are the *kafejnicas*, which can range from greasy spoons to cafeterias and coffee houses.

With Riga's abundance of green spaces and parks, especially adjacent to the Old Town, one should take advantage of a sunny afternoon for a 'picnic in the park'. Start at the central market, just south of the bus station, and pick out a nice selection of breads, cheeses, meats, salads, pastries and drinks, and then stroll a short distance to the banks of the canal, find a quiet spot and enjoy a leisurely lunch.

● *There's plenty of upmarket dining – at a price*

Entertainment & nightlife

Riga is quickly gaining a reputation for having the liveliest nightlife in the Baltic region. The city is almost overflowing with discos, casinos and cabarets. You'll have no difficulty finding something to suit your individual taste, from techno to disco to jazz. And don't assume you have to be under 25 to enjoy Riga's night scene; you'll find plenty of hot spots for those with a more mature outlook on life.

If there's a national pastime in Latvia it must be beer drinking. The most popular brand is Aldaris, followed by Cesu, Uszavas, Pielbalgas and Tervetes.

Filling out the beverage field of competitors is black balsam (see page 28), a good cure for stomach aches and hangovers. Be very wary of *kandza*, a traditional moonshine.

Nightlife in Riga is truly not so different from anywhere else. You can find large, noisy taverns filled with stag parties from the UK bellowing 'Oi!' at regular intervals, or quiet, cosy cocktail bars. There are electric casinos and small bridge clubs, as well as all sorts of other entertainment, from traditional live theatre to cutting-edge independent films at small art theatres.

Despite the influx of techno music and cheap drinking establishments, Riga remains a curiously formal place at night. If you are heading out to drink, eschew the sweatsuits and trainers and at least make an attempt to be chic.

● *Riga lives up to its reputation as the nightlife capital of the Baltic States*

Sport & relaxation

Exercise, fitness and sports are big in Latvia, with the country bringing home many Olympic medals, especially in bobsleigh.

SPECTATOR SPORTS

Apart from winter sports (see pages 12–13), football is the major sport in Latvia, with many players competing at local, national and international levels. The Latvian team surprised many when they qualified for the 2004 European Championships. The national team plays regular matches against Russia and other national teams from countries that border the Baltic. These matches, held in Riga at Skonto Stadium, are well attended. The stadium is about a 15-min walk from the Old Town, and tickets are available at the stadium on match days.

Skonto Stadium ⓐ E Melngaila iela 1a, Riga

ACTIVITIES

Most major hotels offer exercise facilities and swimming pools. The promenades along the Daugava, the green belts around the canal, as well as city parks such as Mezaparks, are good for hiking and jogging. Riga has several clubs that offer aerobics, weight-lifting, yoga and other forms of fitness training. Facilities for basketball, billiards, cycling, horse riding, swimming, skating and tennis are also available in Riga.

At Sigulda, you can bungee jump over the Gauja River from a cable car. The height is about 45 m (148 ft). It operates Saturday and Sunday from 18.30 at a cost of 13 Lats for the first jump, and 11 Lats for subsequent jumps. Call ahead to make sure they are operating when you want to go.

EXERCISE & RELAXATION

If you absolutely, positively cannot go a day without working up a sweat with weights and cardio, don't despair. There are lots of health clubs, most offering aerobic classes, and many of the larger chain hotels are equipped with swimming pools and exercise rooms. What else would you expect? Latvia maybe a small country but it possesses a large number of athletes who have brought home a pile of Olympic gold medals. And if aromatherapy, deep tissue massage and a pedicure are more of your idea of a workout, neither the city or seashore locations will disappoint.

Yoga Centres

City Fitness ⓐ Elizabetes iela 55. ⓣ 777 22 87.

Daya Yoga Studio ⓐ Stabu iela 51/2. ⓣ 655 50 60.

Shakti Ayurveda centre, lessons, pancharkarma and ayurvedic massage. ⓐ Adujela iela 8, 2nd floor. ⓣ 972 61 58. ⓦ www.shakti.lv

Health Clubs

Centrs ⓐ Adeju iela 16. ⓣ 701 80 00.

City Fitness Yoga, pilates, ballet, spinning, rowing, sauna and massage. ⓐ Elizabetes iela 55. ⓣ 777 22 87.

Radisson Wellness Centre Pool, sauna, spa, hairdresser, exercise studio. ⓐ Radisson Hotel, Kugu iela 24. ⓣ 706 11 11. ⓦ www.radissonsas.com

Accommodation

Riga has a wide range of hotels, bed and breakfasts, and some hostels, but any of these will take a significant chunk out of your budget. Latvia has not yet adopted the international 5-star standards so relying strictly on this as an indicator of the quality of the establishment may not be the best idea. Always be sure to ask what will be included with the room if items such as bathtubs or satellite TV service are a priority for your stay. Many mid-price hotels are former Soviet establishments and the furnishings and amenities usually haven't been updated for quite some time. Outside the city, guest houses or *viesu names* are springing up like poppies after rain.

HOSTELS

Argonaut Hostel £ You can choose from dorm rooms, singles or doubles in this Old City hostel just a stone's throw from the bus station, and within stumbling distance of some very good pubs. Rooms are fresh and clean, internet access is available, and there is no curfew. ❷ Kaleju iela 50. ❶ 614 72 14. ❶ 727 88 09.

Elizabeth's Youth Hostel £ Conveniently located near both the bus and train stations, this hostel is clean and comfortable. A common room with TV, free internet access, refrigerator and microwave is available.

PRICE RATING
The following price guides are based on the cost of a room for two people including breakfast, per night.
£ Under £20. **££** £20–40. **£££** £40–80. **£££+** Over £80.

Dorms and doubles available. ⓐ Elizabetes iela 101.
ⓣ 670 54 76.

BED & BREAKFAST

Homestay £ This bright and inviting home in the Mezaparks area, run by a Latvian-New Zealand couple, is both comfy and hospitable. Guests have access to the kitchen, the living room with its multi-channel television, English books in every room, and a shower with skylights. ⓐ Stokholmas iela 1. ⓣ/ⓕ 727 02 65. Ⓥ Take Tram no. 11, or call them to arrange transportation.

Lenz Bed and Breakfast £ Located within easy distance of the city's impressive art nouveau district, this B&B offers bright and spacious rooms spread over three floors. The bathrooms and kitchen are shared. Also available is a computer with internet access.
ⓐ Lencu iela 2. ⓣ 733 33 43. ⓕ 733 13 78.

Serena ££ This little bed and breakfast in the Old Town offers four rooms with large beds, satellite TV, minibar, writing desk and private bathrooms with shower. Good location from which to begin your sightseeing. ⓐ Jekaba iela 26/28. ⓣ 732 45 45.

HOTELS

Livonija £ A cosy little motel near the Central Market, only a few tram stops from the sightseeing delights of the Old Town. The rooms are a little on the small side but are cheerily decorated. All have private bathrooms and cable TV. An added bonus is the restaurant that serves reasonably priced Latvian food and will deliver to your room if you are just too tired to go downstairs. ⓐ Maskavas 32. ⓣ 720 41 80.
ⓕ 720 41 89.

Saulite £ Located across the street from the rail station, this recently renovated hotel has TV, phones, and private bathrooms with showers. Not luxurious or stylish, but the price is reasonable given the location. ⓐ Merkeja 12. ❶ 722 82 19. ❶ 722 36 29.

Viesnica £ A small (10-room) inn in a quiet location but only about 10 minutes drive from the city centre. Facilities are en-suite and there is a sauna at the hotel, too. ⓐ Caka iela 126. ❶ 750 67 00. ❶ 750 67 01.

Valnis £–££ The passé communist-style decor will reinforce that this establishment was once a hotel for the Ministry of Education in Soviet times. But the rooms are clean and spacious and include a TV, refrigerator, writing desk, private bathroom and narrow beds. Located in Old Riga next to the Powder Tower. ⓐ Vajnu 2. ❶ 721 37 85.

Avitar ££–£££ Cozy, quiet and centrally located. This building was originally intended to house apartments so the rooms are more spacious than normal. They are equipped with refrigerators, telephone and cable TV, and you have the added bonus of shuttle services to the airport, central train or bus station. Breakfast and VAT included. ⓐ K. Valdemara iela 127 ❶ 736 44 44. ❶ 736 49 88. ⓦ www.avitar@apollo.lv

Boutique Hotel Ainavas £££ An intimate and stylish boutique hotel located in the Old Town. Down duvets, heated floors, satellite TV, virtual office for the business traveller and a cosy lounge with a fireplace and bar for romantics. ⓐ Peldu iela 23. ❶ 781 43 16. ❶ 781 43 17.

◗ *Many of the best-value hotels are in the suburbs*

Elizabetes Nams (Elizabeth's House) £££ An intimate hotel within the art nouveau district of the city. The hotel was built in the style of a traditional 18th-century home. Recently renovated, the rooms are all of a different design featuring such touches as bidet, hairdryer, TV and telephone. Prices include breakfast and VAT.
ⓐ Elizabetes iela 27. ❶ 750 92 91. ⓦ www.elizabetesnams.lv

Forums £££ Located in the historical district of the Old Town, the hotel offers double and even triple rooms. Some of the suites have balconies with a fantastic view of the Old Town.
ⓐ Valnu iela 45. ❶ 781 46 80. ❶ 781 46 82.
ⓦ www.hotelforums.lv

Serena £££ Enter this pension-style hotel via a courtyard. Each room has a full range of amenities including mini-bar and bathrobes. Friendly, pleasant and situated in the Old Town for easy sightseeing. Breakfast included. ⓐ Jekaba iela 26–28. ❶/❶ 732 45 45.
ⓔ serena@allhotels.lv

Hotel Gutenbergs £££ An Old Town hotel with a split personality. The newer wing has an intimate air with wooden ceilings and rustic interior, while the old wing maintains its classic and conventional style. All the rooms have cable TV and private bathrooms with hairdryers. Wheelchair access and allergy-free rooms are available. The hotel also features a superb roof terrace restaurant. Pricey, but excellent. ⓐ Doma laukums 1. ❶ 781 40 90. ❶ 750 33 26.

Reval Hotel Ridzene (City Centre) £££ Like a hotel with an eye for detail and a sense of humour? Rooms have cherry wood decorations and a bright yellow rubber duck in each bath. A sauna and fitness suite on the top floor offer a 180-degree view of the city, allowing you to drink in some sights while you sweat away your jet lag. 🄰 Reimersa 1. ☎ 732 44 33. 🖷 732 26 00.

Koventa Seta £££+ This 13th-century convent situated in the very heart of the Old Town has had a multi-purpose past, from its beginnings as a convent to warehouses, apartments and now a hotel. The nine authentic medieval buildings have been renovated to incorporate rooms, conference centre, restaurant and even a museum in the basement. 🄰 Kaleju iela 9–11. ☎ 708 75 01. 🖷 708 75 06. 🄴 reservation@konventa.lv

Vecriga £££+ A romantic, yet modern, sanctuary set amid the antiquity of Old Town. Just 10 spacious and comfortable rooms means you need to book early to secure a space. 🄰 Glexnotaju iela 12/14 (Old Riga). ☎ 721 60 37. 🖷 721 45 61. 🄴 vecriga@inet.ov.

Centra Hotel £££+ Great location for enjoying the pub life and sightseeing of the Old Town. The rooms are small but the service is friendly and you can't beat the location. Ask for one of the rooms on the third or fourth floor, which are adorned with opulent high ceilings. Price includes buffet breakfast and VAT. 🄰 Audeju iela 1. ☎ 722 64 41. 🖷 750 32 81. 🖳 www.centra.lv

Grand Palace £££+ Very expensive. However, if you yearn to stay where the likes of Sting and Catherine Deneuve lodge in Riga, this is the place. The rooms are lavishly decorated in blue, white and gold and are truly fit for a queen or a rock star. 🄰 Pils 12. ☎ 704 40 00. 🖷 704 40 04.

THE BEST OF RIGA

There's plenty to fill a few days and more in Riga itself, and if you use it as a base for seeing the countryside, seashore and cities of the rest of Latvia you can count on easily filling a couple of weeks.

TOP 10 ATTRACTIONS
These are sights you should try not to miss on any trip to Riga.

- **Old Town** Eight centuries of history crammed into a charming chaos of narrow streets adorned with outdoor cafés, intriguing architecture and ultra-hip nightlife (see pages 60–81).

- **Art nouveau architecture** Can't get enough of caryatids and nymphs adorning the architecture? You'll revel in the well-preserved buildings of Riga's art nouveau district, one of the biggest collections in Europe (see pages 86–90).

- **Dome Cathedral** The largest place of worship in the Baltics and housing one of the biggest pipe organs in Europe (see page 73).

- **St Peter's Church** A graceful three-tiered spire adorns this red-brick church. Climb to the top for a jaw-dropping view of the Old Town and environs (see pages 68–70).

- **House of the Blackheads** Weird name, but this reconstructed medieval structure is the showpiece of the Old Town (see pages 65–67).

- **Central Market** On its completion in 1930, Riga's Central Market was one of the largest and most modern in Europe. Visit it to sample an authentic slice of Latvian life (see pages 91–92).

- **Open-air Ethnographic Museum** Spend a while in an atmosphere of days gone by in this vast ensemble of timber-built farmhouses garnered from all regions of the country (see page 93).

- **Jurmala** This stretch of seashore, only a short distance from Riga, is the bucket-and-spade paradise of Latvia (see pages 102–109).

- **Gaujas National Park** A spectacularly beautiful national park in Eastern Latvia. Canoeing the Gauja River is one of Latvia's most popular recreational activities (see pages 118–120).

- **Rundale Palace** Go for baroque! This sumptuous palace is simply stuffed with rococo furnishings. A true monument to the excesses of 18th-century aristocrats (see page 130).

▼ *Rigas Pils dominates the north bank of the Daugava*

Here's a quick guide to the best that a visit to Riga can offer, depending on how much time you have available.

HALF-DAY: RIGA IN A HURRY

If your time for sightseeing is limited to only a few hours, you are in luck. Riga, especially the historic Old Town, is quite compact, with many of the city's top attractions bunched quite close together. So put on your walking shoes and go (see pages 60–81). Start at Ratslaukums (Town Hall Square) and even if you confine your exploration to the immediate surrounding area, ending up at the cathedral in Doma laukums, you'll easily fill a morning or afternoon.

ONE DAY: TIME TO SEE A LITTLE MORE

With a whole day to spare, you can widen your horizons after the whistle-stop tour suggested above, and explore more of Riga's historic centre. If you still have a little time to spare, check out Riga's Central Market just over the railway tracks.

If you have survived this expedition, you have seen most of the best of the Old Town. Go and join the locals for a beer.

2–3 DAYS: SHORT CITY-BREAK

If you have more than one day, and have been concentrating on the Old Town, you should take a look at some of the other things Riga has to offer. If you want to slow down the pace, try exploring the city's parks, beyond Brivibas bulvaris and the Freedom Monument. If you haven't already investigated the city's art nouveau architecture, follow our itinerary on pages 86–90 around the small area near Elizabetes iela that has the greatest concentration of art nouveau buildings in the city, if not the world.

If you enjoy things mechanical, try the Latvian Railway Museum (about 1 km across the Akmens tilts bridge in western Riga) or the Motor Museum (see page 93), also a little out of town. For those with green fingers, Riga has the Botanical Gardens in Pardaugava and Salaspils, the site of the Latvian National Botanical Gardens.

LONGER: ENJOYING RIGA TO THE FULL

If you find yourself with at least a week in Riga, you should consider travelling out to see more of Latvia on one or two of our suggested Out of Town trips. Just north-west of Riga is Jurmala (Seashore), a collection of small beach resorts scattered along about 20 km (12 miles) of the Baltic coastline. This is a good half-day excursion, or you can arrange for a hotel room and spend a whole day at the beach.

Bauska is about 75 km (46 miles) south of Riga. The ruins of Bauska Castle, currently undergoing reconstruction, are worth a visit, while 13 km (8 miles) west is Rundale Palace, a magnificent baroque structure filled with rococo furnishings and 10 km (6 miles) north-west is Mezotne Palace, a neo-classical building. You should plan on a full day to see all three sites.

In the east of Latvia are the Gauja Valley, with the Gaujas National Park, and the towns of Sigulda and Cesis. The area is also laced with the remains of old Livonian castles, churches and museums. It would easily take two or three days to explore this area and to admire its natural beauty.

To the west are the Baltic Coast, and the towns of Kuldiga (the prettiest of the provincial towns in Latvia) and seaside Ventspils and Liepaja. If there has been a recent storm, look for amber washed up on the seashore. This is at least a two-day trip, but you may want to take longer.

Something for nothing

You don't have to spend a fortune to enjoy much of what Riga has to offer. Here are just a few ideas for getting the most out of a visit without denting your wallet.

The Old Town
There is no charge for the history that you cannot help but absorb as you wander the chaotic mass of streets and statuary (see pages 60–81)

Latvian History Museum
On Wednesdays wander through halls of history at this museum – it's free! And you'll learn a little bit about Latvian history to boot (see page 73).

● There is no charge for exploring Riga's fascinating streets and squares

Bralu kapi (Brethren Cemetery)
Designed by Latvian sculptor Karlis Zale, this is truly one of the most striking memorials in Latvia. It was built as a tribute to the 2000 soldiers who fell during World Wars I and II. ❸ Berzu alega.

Museum of Latvia's Occupation
This museum is worthy of its admission price any day,

so take advantage of this freebie. The various exhibits display the atrocities committed against the Latvian people. You can even walk into a reconstruction of a gulag barracks and get a sense of the intolerable living conditions of a Siberian labour camp (see pages 62, 68).

Aviation Museum

One of the richest collections of aircraft in Eastern Europe is assembled in this building adjacent to the passenger terminal at the airport. It includes war, passenger, sport and training planes, as well as helicopters. A special treat is the display of almost all the models of the famous Soviet MiGs, including the world's fastest warplane, the MiG25. ❷ Riga Airport. ❶ 686 27 07. ❸ 10.00–17.00, closed Sat and Sun.

Kreisais Pagrieziens

A stylish club that draws both local and European artists such as Marija Naumova. Lots of 'unplugged' concerts are recorded here, so be prepared to be a hushed and respectful audience during a taping. ❷ Kalku 11a. ❶ 721 25 75. ❶ 721 25 75. ❸ 20.00–01.00 Tues, Wed 20.00–05.00 Thur–Sat, closed Sun–Mon.

Bird watching

Located along the flight path of the north-south migration routes, the Baltic States play host to a wide variety of feathered visitors. Most visible are the white storks which arrive every spring and immediately set up camp atop roofs and telegraph poles all over the region. Coastal areas and fish-laden wetland areas attract many species including cranes, mute swans and several varieties of geese. In Estonia prime locations include Lahemaa National Park, Vilsandi National Park and the Matsula Nature Preserve.

When it rains

Riga may be one of the best cities in which to spend a drizzly day, which is a very good thing because it certainly does drizzle a lot here. Fortunately, there are enough museums and cinemas to satisfy cravings for an historic or contemporary culture fix. The smaller museums reveal a close-up look at the Latvian personality and the need to document, it would seem, everything. Here are some of the best.

Menzendorff House (see page 74) offers a glimpse of how wealthy Rigensians lived in the 17th and 18th centuries. Once owned by a rich merchant, this museum provides a glimpse of the day-to-day life of that era.

The creepy-crawlies at the **Museum of Nature** (see page 92) include everything from specimens from the Cretaceous era to pickled body parts. It also has the best collection of fossilised fish in the former USSR.

The impressive exterior of **House of the Blackheads** is matched by the opulent rooms inside (see page 65).

Porcelana Galerija (Porcelain Gallery) More than just a gallery for contemporary Latvian porcelain artists, this is a creative space where you can paint your own cup or plate. Enter via the bookstore in the House of the Blackheads. ⓐ Svaru iela 3/5. ⓣ 704 43 78.

Seno Spekratu Izstade (Motor Museum) Can't get enough of chrome and running-boards? Spend an afternoon away from the city in this exhibition of classic cars. Lincolns, Mercedes and BMWs are all garaged together along with some motorcycles (some with sidecars) from days gone by (see page 93).

◗ *Head for the House of the Blackheads when rain threatens*

On arrival

TIME DIFFERENCES

Latvia is 2 hours ahead of Greenwich Mean Time (GMT) and 3 hours ahead during daylight savings.

ARRIVING

By air

Riga International Airport is located 13 km (8 miles) south-west of Riga centre. The airport was recently given an award for being the best airport of its size in the EU. The airport has a full range of services from money exchange, tourist information, banks, internet services, post office, rental car services, shops and restaurants.

Bus no. 22 goes to the city centre (Strelnieku laukums and the train station) and leaves every 20–30 minutes. The cost is 0.20L.

You can order a taxi from a desk in the arrivals hall, or you can simply go outside and hail one from a queue of eager taxis waiting outside the arrivals hall. A typical ride to Old Riga or the city centre should cost no more than 10L. It is recommended to take a licensed taxi – one which is clearly marked and in which there is a meter. Some hotels provide a free shuttle service from the airport.

Riga International Airport 🆆 www.riga-airport.com

By rail

The main rail station is located adjacent to the south end of the Old Town, and is also close to the city centre. There are separate arrival and departure lounges for domestic and international services. The station has an ATM, currency exchange, information, post office, ticket booths and restaurants. Taxis are available outside the station.

Central Railway Station 🅰 Stacijas laukums. 🆃 117, 118. Information about international railway routes: 723 28 20, 723 30 95. Ticket booking: 721 66 64, 583 33 97. Ⓦ www.ldz.lv

By bus

Riga is connected by bus lines to most major cities in Europe. The bus station is located on the Riga Canal at the south end of the Old Town. It has ticket booths, currency exchange, ATM, internet access, a drug store, a news-stand and a cafeteria.

A bridge across the Riga Canal leads to the Rail station. Tram 7 stops in front of the bus station, and will take you into the centre of town for 0.20 Lats. Taxis are also available outside.

Riga International Bus Station ⓐ Pragas iela 1, Riga, LV-1050. Ⓦ www.autoosta.lv

By ferry

There are limited international ferry services from Kiel and Lübeck in Germany, and from Stockholm, Sweden. Riga's Sea Passenger Terminal is about 1 km from the Old Town. The terminal has currency exchange and a restaurant. Trams no. 5, 7 or 9 all stop in front of the terminal, and will take you to the city centre for 0.20 Lats. Taxis are available outside the terminal.

Riga Sea Passenger Terminal ⓐ Eksporta iela 3a, Riga, LV-1010. ❶ 732 62 00. ❶ 732 61 95.

By road

Riga is served by highways to the north, east and south. Highway E67 goes north to Estonia, and south to Lithuania; Highway E77 and Highway E22 both go east to Russia; Highway A6 goes south-east to Belarus; and Highway E66 goes south-west to Lithuania. The highways are maintained to good standards.

Speed limits are 50 km/h in towns, 70 km/h in suburbs, 90 km/h on open roads, and 110 km/h on highways. As in the rest of continental Europe, driving is on the right-hand side. Seat-belt use is mandatory. There is zero tolerance for the use of alcohol while driving, and use of mobile phones while driving is also forbidden. It is also compulsory to drive with headlights on from the beginning of October until the end of March. Foreign drivers are required to have a national licence, an International Driving Permit, registration documents, and proof of insurance.

FINDING YOUR FEET

If you are going to be in Riga for one to three days, and plan to see as many sights as possible, it is recommended that you buy a **Riga Card**. A sightseeing tour, entrance to most cultural and tourist attractions, and entry to most museums is included in the price of the card. You can also use it as a transport ticket on trams and trolleybuses. Some merchants also offer discounts on goods and services to holders of valid Riga Cards. The cost of the card is 8L for 24 hours, 12 Lats for 48 hours, and 16 Lats for 72 hours. Children under the age of 16 are half price.

You can buy the Riga Card at the Riga Tourist Information Centre, ⓐ Ratslaukums 6, or at the following travel agencies: Latvia Tours ⓐ Kalku iela 8; and Eurotravel ⓐ Lecplesa iela 29.

Information is available at: ⓔinfo@rigacard.lv; and ⓣ 721 7217. Make your first stop the tourist information centre in the Old Town. It offers a wide range of information in a variety of languages and can assist with hotel bookings and other useful services. This is also an excellent place to buy your Riga Card.

City of Riga Information Centre ⓐ Ratslaukums 6. ⓣ 704 43 77. ⓕ 704 43 78. ⓦ www.rigatourism.com

With Independence well established, help from IMF loans, and entry into the EU, the Latvian economy is booming and Riga is at the centre of that boom. Despite this, wealth is still concentrated among the few, with many residents struggling to make ends meet. Although the overall crime rate is low, petty theft is a problem. Stealing from hotel rooms, especially the cheaper ones, is common. Sneak thieves and pickpockets are also common, especially in areas frequented by tourists. Visitors would be well advised not to carry large sums of cash, and not to flaunt expensive jewellery, cameras or electronic equipment. Such items are better left at home unless really needed. Riga also has its share of muggers, so beware of dark areas, especially at night and near drinking establishments. If possible, do not walk alone.

Traffic in Riga is bad, and the driving tends to be aggressive and definitely not pedestrian-friendly. You need to be careful when crossing streets. Drunken driving is also common.

The pace of life is quite hectic in Riga, except in the Old Town. Here, the narrow winding streets are not conducive to cars – few are present, and those that do enter must pay a fee. With most of the Old Town reserved for pedestrians, everything seems to run at a much more leisurely and relaxed pace.

English is not as widely spoken in Latvia as in many other European countries, a result of many years behind the Iron Curtain. However, more Latvians, especially those in international business and those in the tourist industry, are learning to speak it. There is one English- language newspaper in Latvia; *The Baltic Times* is published weekly, and is available at most hotels, some restaurants, and many news-stands. Other English-language publications are shipped into Riga, and, again, are available at most major hotels, and at many news-stands.

ORIENTATION

Riga sits on the Daugava River, about 10 km (6 miles) from the mouth of the river which empties into the south part of Riga Bay. The eastern, or right, bank holds most of the interesting parts of Riga. The historic heart of the city, the Old Town (Old Riga or Vecriga), is about 1.5 km (1 mile) long by about 1km (0.6 miles) wide, and is surrounded by the Daugava River to the south-west, and by the Pilsetas Kanals (City Canal) to the north-west.

11 Novembra krastmala is a wide street that runs along the west side of the Old Town, and there is a wide pedestrian walkway on the river side of 11 Novembra. The skyline of the Old Town is dominated by four spires: from north to south these are St Jakob's Church, the Dome Cathedral, the clock tower of the Town Hall, and St Peter's Church.

The Old Town is bisected by Kalku iela. About a block from the river on Kalku iela is Ratslaukums, or Town Square. The Ratsnams (Town Hall), the Blackheads House, the Museum of the Occupation, and a very good tourist information office are located at Ratslaukums. The main railway station and the main international bus terminal are on the south-east edge of the Old Town.

The rest of the 'new' city radiates outwards from the Old Town. At the Canal, Kalku becomes Brivibas bulvaris. To the north side of Brivibas is the area containing art nouveau architecture, and to the south is the State University. The western, or left, bank of the Daugava River is the site of Riga International Airport. It is generally an industrial area, and of little interest to visitors.

An outstanding place to begin getting a sense of Riga, especially if you've never been here before, is from atop the sky-scraping Reval Hotel Latvija at Elizabetes iela 55; by looking out of the tall windows on both sides of the eagle's nest Skyline Bar, you can see virtually the whole of the city.

IF YOU GET LOST, TRY ...

Excuse me, do you speak English?
Atvainojiet, vai jūs runājat angliski?
Atvainoyiet, vai yus runayat angliski?

**Excuse me, is this the right way to the cathedral/the tourist
information office/the castle/the old town?**
Atvainojiet, vai šis ir pareizais ceļš uz katedrāli/
tūristu informācijas biroju/baznīcu/vecpilsētu?
*Atvainoyiet, vai shis ir pareizais celysh uz katedrali/turistu
informatsiyas biroyu/baznitsu/vetspilsetu?*

Can you point to it on my map?
Vai jūs varētu to parādīt uz manas kartes?
Vai yus varetu to paradit uz manas kartes?

GETTING AROUND

On foot Riga is quite compact, with most major attractions within
1 km (0.6 miles) of the City Centre and Old Town, so walking is a
practical and viable option. The maps in this book are up to date and
will help you navigate the main streets, but Riga's street system is
complex and a detailed map obtained locally will be invaluable.

Public transport

Riga has an extensive network of trams, buses, trolleys and local
trains. The cost is only 0.20 Lats for any one trip, but there are no
transfers. Tickets may be purchased from the driver or conductor.

Taxis

There are several taxi companies in Riga, and it is easy to flag down a taxi. There are still some taxis that are less than honest. Be sure the taxi is properly marked, and that it has a visible meter, and that the driver uses it. Reputable taxis are **Bona-M** (❶ 800 50 50), **Riga Taxi** (❶ 800 10 10 or 800 00 06) and **Rigas Taksometru parks** (❶ 800 1313). A taxi ride to and from any point inside the city centre/Old Town area should cost about 3L to 5L. Rates are slightly higher at night. Some taxis are now taking some credit cards, so look for your card's sticker in the window.

CAR HIRE

Unless you are planning on visiting locations well outside of Riga, renting a car is not recommended. The city is compact, with most of the attractions close enough, that walking, using public transport, or even hiring taxis, is much more economical and practical. However most of the major car rental agencies are represented in Riga, both at the airport, and in the city centre. You can expect to pay the same prices as in Western Europe. There are some local car rental companies that can be cheaper than the major renters, but the mechanical condition of the car, as well as any insurance that may be on it, is often questionable. Some major car rental agencies in Riga are:

Avis ❶ 722 58 76. ⓦ www.avis.lv

Budget ❶ 720 73 27. ⓦ www.budget.lv

Europcar ❶ 722 26 37. ⓦ www.europcar.lv

Hertz ❶ 730 77 10, 722 42 23. ⓦ www.hertz.lv

---

❶ *Riga Old Town is ringed by parks and open spaces*

Old Town

The Old Town, the historic and geographic centre of the city, is located on the right bank of the Daugava River. Built between the 13th and 18th centuries, it contains a unique collection of architectural monuments and buildings. A walk through its cobble-stoned streets will make you feel as if you have journeyed back in time.

Start at Ratslaukums (Town Hall Square), where you get to see four sights in one. First is the House of the Blackheads. This building is a reconstruction of the original building which was completely destroyed in World War II. Riga's main tourist office is located here and can give you maps and other information to make the rest of your sightseeing easier. You can also buy your Riga Card here.

The House of the Blackheads was started in the 14th century, and over the years evolved into the centre of business and music. For centuries it was the heart of both the business and social life of the city. Today, chamber concerts are still held in the main hall.

Across the street is Ratsnams (Town Hall). It too was destroyed in World War II. Rebuilt by the Russians after the war as a soviet-style block, it has been completely redone since Independence. Although a modern office building on the inside, the outside has been desipned in an attractive neo-classical style, complete with clock tower.

On the square between Ratsnams and the House of the Blackheads is a stature of Roland, the legendary 8th-century knight who was killed fighting the Moors in a battle for control of a Pyrenean mountain pass. The first statue was erected in the 14th century on this same spot and it has been replaced many times since, the current version being a copy of one from the 19th century.

Esplanade

K. Valdemara iela

Kalpaka bulvaris

Kronvalda bulvaris

Raina bulvaris

Valdemara iela

Jekaba iela

Jekaba laukums

Pilsetas Kanals

Bastion Hill

Freedom Monument

Torna iela

St. James' Barracks

Swedish Gate

Pils laukums

Jekaba iela

Aldan iela

Powder Tower

Basteja bulvaris

St Jakob's Church

Maza Pils iela

Smilsu iela

Brivibas bulvaris

Pils iela

Three Brothers

Great Guild

Livu laukums

Aspazijas bulvaris

St Saviours

Doma laukums

Meistau iela

Kalku iela

Valnu iela

Kaleju iela

Small Guild

Central Station

Dome Cathedral

Kaleju iela

Riga History Museum

Ratsnams

Skarnu iela

Museum of Decorative & Applied Arts

Ratslaukums

Kungu iela

St. Peter's Church

St. John's Church

Centrs

Kalku iela

Grecinieku iela

Valnu iela

Museum of Latvia's Occupation

House of the Blackheads

UGAVA

11. Novembra krastmala

Kungu iela

13. janvara iela

Akmens tilts

N

250m   500m

On the west side of Ratslaukums is the rear of the Museum of Latvia's Occupation. It is a squat, black, forbidding structure, which contrasts sharply with the colourful buildings around it. The museum was built by the Russians to honour the Latvian Riflemen, a group of Latvian soldiers who fought bravely for the Bolsheviks during the Russian Civil War, and who were used to execute the Russian royal family. Since Independence, the museum has been converted to show the horrors endured by the Latvians at the hands of both the Germans and Russians since the beginning of World War II. Entry is on the west side of the building off Latviesu Strelnieku laukums (Latvian Riflemen's Square). The square also has a monument to the riflemen.

From Ratslaukums, walk east in front of the House of the Blackheads, cross Kungu iela, and you will be at St Peter's Church. This large red-brick church has a graceful three-tiered spire which is the city's trademark symbol. The original spire was built in 1491, but collapsed 200 years later has been rebuilt and destroyed several times, most recently by German bombs in 1941. The current spire is 123 m (403 ft) high and has an internal elevator which will take you to an observation tower for an impressive view of the entire city.

Due east of St Peter's Church, on Skarnu iela, is St John's Church. Built in the 13th century, the red and green brick gable looks best in the afternoon sun. The Gothic interior has recently been painted in bright primary colours.

Moving north-west on Skarnu iela, you come to the 13th-century chapel of St George, which now houses the Museum of Decorative and Applied Arts, which displays such things as weaving, glassware, pottery and tableware.

Continue north-west on Skarnu iela, turn right on Kalku iela and

---

⬤ *Roland has been keeping watch on the Town Hall for centuries*

left one block later onto Meistaru iela. This brings you to Livu laukums, where you will find clustered together two buildings known as the Great Guild and Small Guild. The neo-Gothic Great Guild was given its current appearance in the 19th century, and now serves as a venue for performances of the Latvian National Symphony Orchestra. The Small Guild is more interesting, being asymmetrical with a turret on one side and a spire on the other. Facing the guilds is a yellow building in art nouveau style, with cats decorating its two turrets, and hence called the House of the Cats.

Continuing north on Meistaru, you will come to the Pulvertornis, or Powder Tower. This red-brick bastion was built in the 14th century. Its walls are embedded with cannonballs from various sieges. It is now part of the Latvian War Museum.

From the north side of the Powder Tower, go west on Torna iela. The long building on the north side of the street is St James's Barracks. Originally built by the Swedes in the 17th century, it now contains offices and upmarket shops. At Aldaru iela you will see the Swedish Gate. It is a simple archway beneath a large house, and is

PILSETAS KANAL

The Old Town was a fortified city for many years, with a moat around it. In the middle of the 19th century, it was decided it was no longer necessary to fortify the city, and many buildings and ramparts were dismantled. With so much open area, green spaces, and parks 300 m (984 ft) wide or more, were created on both sides of the canal. Public buildings were also added to the area. Today this space provides an oasis in the middle of this modern and growing city.

the only surviving city gate. It no longer goes anywhere in particular, but the alleys on the other side make an interesting side trip.

Continuing along Torna iela, you will come to Jekaba laukums. Across from the square is the Arsenal Gallery, which features high-profile contemporary art shows. Torna iela ends at Pils laukums, the site of Rigas Pils (Riga Castle). Originally built in the 13th century as headquarters for the Livonian Order, the castle has been through several alterations. Today it is the official residence of the Latvian president, as well as the home of three museums, the Foreign Art Museum, the Latvian History Museum and the Museum of Writing, Theatre and Music. From the south end of Pils laukums, go east on Maza Pils iela. Here you will find three interesting buildings known as the Three Brothers. The first dates back to 1400 and appears to be falling over. It has a wild and crazy paint scheme. The second brother is painted yellow, and has an interesting portal. It houses the Latvian Architecture Museum. The third brother is rather unassuming, and painted green. At the end of Maza Pils iela, turn right on Jekaba iela, and you will come to Doma laukums (Cathedral Square).

Doma laukums is the core of the Old Town, and a good place to end a half-day tour. The square is dominated by Riga's Romanesque cathedral; begun in 1211, it is the biggest cathedral in the Baltics. It is magnificent both inside and out. The cathedral features a huge organ (within 6768 pipes) constructed in the 19th century. The largest in the world when built, it is now ranked fourth largest.

SIGHTS & ATTRACTIONS

House of the Blackheads

This is one of the best-known architectural treasures of Riga. Original construction began in the 14th century on the two

buildings that comprise an asymmetrical and somewhat incongruous structure. The building boasts enormous stepped gables, ornately framed windows and niches filled with statuary. Initially the house was used as a meeting place for many of Riga's guilds. Eventually it become associated with just one group – the unmarried merchants who took the name Blackheads in honour of their patron St Maurice, a Roman warrior of North African origin, . Over the centuries the building was the scene of rowdy, grandiose feasts such as Fasnachtsdrunken (Carnival Drinking Bout), debuts of musical works and theatrical events. Very nearly bombed into extinction during World War II, the buildings have been meticulously restored to their former glory.

The Blackheads survived as an organisation until 1940, when the last of its members were repatriated to Germany with the rest of Latvia's Germans. Today the House fulfils a social role in the city, serving as a venue for chamber music concerts, and sharing ground-level space with the Riga tourist office and a café styled in the opulence of the 19th century.

ⓐ Ratslaukums 7. ⓣ 704 43 00. ⓛ 10.00–17.00, closed Mon. Admission charge. ⓝ Trolleybus 6, 8 or 9.

Ratslaukums (Town Hall Square) & Statue of Roland

In the 14th century statues of Roland began appearing all over northern Germany as a symbol of justice and freedom. He was considered to be a just judge and defender of the accused, and so his statue was placed in the Town Hall Square in front of the Guilds of Hanseatic cities. The point of Roland's sword was the spot from which distances were measured in Riga and Latvia.

ⓞ *St Maurice guards one side of the entrance to the House of the Blackheads*

Museum of Latvia's Occupation

Once solely devoted to honouring the Latvian Red Riflemen, the building now houses a museum dedicated to the Nazi and Soviet occupations of Latvia. Various exhibits display the atrocities committed against the people of Latvia and the attempted systematic destruction of the nation's sovereignty. Visitors can walk into a reconstruction of a gulag barrack and glimpse the intolerable living conditions of those cruelly sentenced to one of these labour camps.

ⓐ Strelnieku laukums 1. ① 721 27 15. ⓛ 11.00–17.00. Closed Mon. Free admission. Ⓝ Bus 21, 22 or 23; trolleybus 3, 13, 15 or 18; tram 3, 6, 7, 8, 10 or 13.

Latvian Riflemen Memorial

In the heart of the Old Town stands a somewhat controversial statue honouring the Latvian Red Riflemen, some of whom became the personal guards of Lenin. Some residents of the city see this monument as a symbol of the Soviet occupation and yearn to tear it down. Others see it as a tribute to the Latvians who fought in the early years of World War I. Regardless of which side you take, it is an impressive statue.

ⓐ Strelnieku laukums 1.

St Peter's Church

This 13th-century church was ruined during World War II and repaired during the Soviet occupation. A 360-degree platform around the spire allows you to view all of Riga and the Old Town – a perfect way to get your bearings and plan your sightseeing.

⊙ *The Riflemen's Memorial is a controversial legacy of Soviet days*

ⓐ Skarnu iela 19. ☎ 722 94 26. 🕐 10.00–17.00. Closed Mon. Admission charge.

Great & Small Guild Halls

The Great Guild Hall was once home to Riga's power brokers, the merchants, while the Small Guild was for the city's artisans. Today these two 14th-century buildings are venues for musical performances. The Great Guild is home to the Philharmonic Orchestra and the smaller cousin hosts contemporary performances and conferences.

ⓐ Amatu iela 6 & 5. Philharmonic Orchestra: ☎ 721 36 43.

Kaku maja (House of the Cats)

Rejected from a guild? Want to get even? Commission a pair of statuary cats to perch atop your roof with their backsides positioned in the direction of those who rejected you. That's the course the owner of this house took to show his displeasure at being turned down for guild membership. The guild viewed this action as the insult it was meant to be and sued in court to have the animals shifted to a less offensive position. They won the case.

ⓐ Meistrau.

Pulvertornis (Powder Tower) & Latvian War Museum

One of the city towers that helped to form the city's walled fortifications, the Pulvertornis dates back to 1330. Rebuilt several times, it took on its present identity in the 17th century because gunpowder came to be stored here. A military museum was added in 1919, with new structures attached in 1937 and 1939.

ⓐ Smilsu iela 20. Ⓝ Bus 21, 22 or 32; trolleybus 3, 13, 15 or 18; tram 3, 6, 7, 8, 10 or 13.

> **DID YOU KNOW?**
> Most steeples of Riga churches are topped by gilded cocks.
> Contrary to the sinister biblical significance of this animal, in
> Latvian folklore it stands for vigilance and safeguards from
> evil. When the cock crows for the third time, the devil must
> retreat back to hell. This practice of placing a cock on the spire
> of a church dates from the Middle Ages, when the cock also
> had a practical use as a weather vane.

The Swedish Gate

The last remaining gate of the old city wall, built during the Swedish
reign. During the 1800s Riga's walls were torn down to provide
easier access to the economically booming city.

Rigas Pils (Riga Castle)

Built in 1330, the Castle was originally constructed to be the
residence for the Grand Master of the Livonian Order. It is now the
official residence of the Latvian president. The president keeps office
in the castle but does not actually live here. The complex also
contains the Foreign Art Museum and the Latvian History Museum.
🅐 Pils laukums. 🚋 Trolleybus 5.

Foreign Art Museum

This museum houses the largest collection of foreign art in Latvia,
with works dating back to the 15th century. Highlights include works
of German and Dutch masters from the 17th to 19th centuries.
📞 722 64 67. 🕐 11.00–17.00. Closed Mon and Thurs.

Latvian History Museum

View the evolution of Latvia and its people from the Stone Age to the present. Themed exhibits include ancient times, medieval Riga, the lifestyle of the peasants and upper classes in the 18th and 19th centuries, the foundation of the Latvian republic and the occupation by the Soviets. Tours are available in English but must be ordered in advance.

❶ 722 13 57. 🕐 11.00–17.00. Closed Mon & Tues. Admission charge (free on Wed).

The Three Brothers

Excellent examples of medieval dwellings. Number 17, built in the 1400s, is the oldest stone house in Latvia. Number 19 houses an architectural museum and number 21 took on its current appearance in the 17th century. Viewed together they constitute almost a textbook of the architectural development of Riga over the centuries.

ⓐ Maza Pils iela 17, 19, 21.

Dome Cathedral

The largest church in Latvia was constructed over several centuries, beginning in 1211, and its architecture reflects a varied mix of early Gothic, baroque and Romanesque styles, among others. Despite the many influences, the structure has an eclectic flair that enchants the eye. The inside of the Cathedral is chock-a-block with plaques commemorating Latvia's medieval rulers. The church organ, the fourth largest in the world, was installed in 1884. Grab a schedule at the entrance or tourist office and make a point of hearing a concert.

◀ *These Three Brothers were born centuries apart*

🅐 Doma laukums 1. ☎ 721 34 98. Admission is charged. NB: at the time of writing the Cathedral was closed to visitors.

Museum of Riga's History & Navigation
This museum leads you through the process of how a small settlement on the bank of the Ridzene River grew into a large Hanseatic city. A good, but sometimes ghoulish, collection that includes a mummified hand and a 16th-century executioner's sword.
🅐 Palasta iela 4. ☎ 721 20 51. 🕐 10.00–17.00.

Big Christopher
Legend has it that Big Christopher, the protector of the city from floods and other natural disasters, first appeared in the 16th century in a small cave in a bank of the Daugava River. For centuries Latvians have paid tribute to this gentle giant with flowers and lit candles, asking for his blessing before departing on a long journey. In modern times his statue was moved to the safety of the Museum of Riga's History and Navigation. Today, a small replica in a glass case stands guard over the river.
🅐 Poju Gate and 11 Novembra krastmala.

Menzendorff House
Wander around the inside of this 17th-century house and discover how Riga's wealthy lived some 300 years ago. The building is filled with antique furniture, frescoes and household items.
🅐 Grecinieku iela v. ☎ 721 29 51. 🕐 11.00–17.00.

St Saviour's Church
A little piece of Britain in Riga's old town. This Gothic-style church

UNDER THE CLOCK

An excellent meeting place is the rectangular clock, advertising Laima Chocolate, on the eastern edge of the Old Town next to the Freedom Monument, where Brivibas iela and Aspazijas bulvaris intersect.

was built in 1857 on 10 m of gravel brought from Britain by a group of English merchants. Services are conducted in English every Sunday at 11.30. ⓐ Anglikanu 2a.

CULTURE

The heart of the Old Town is Dome Square where, in summer, tables and chairs spill out into the area from cafés and bars, creating a fun-filled atmosphere. And when the weather is less cooperative for outdoor festivities folks flock to the interiors of the Opera House, live theatres and restaurants.

Latvian National Theatre A resident company of about 40 actors is devoted to the presentation of Latvian classical plays and the development of original dramas by Latvian playwrights.
ⓐ Kronvalda bulv. 2. ☎ 732 27 59.

Latvian National Opera 'The White House', a magnificent concert hall originally intended to house the City of Riga's German Theatre, was completely renovated in 1995. State-of-the-art technology complements the pristine museum interior of 1862. The opera features world-famous stars as well as rising young talents.

Aspazijas bulv. 3. 707 37 77. 722 89 30. www.opera.lv
 Tram 5, 7 or 9.

Forum Cinemas (Baltic Cinema) With 14 screens this is the second-largest cinema complex in Northern Europe. A bar and café make for a complete evening out. 13 Habvara 8.

Kinogalerija A small movie theatre in the Old Town that shows classics and art films. Bring your own popcorn or drink.
 Jaun iela 24. 722 90 30.

Riga Once called the Splendid Palace, the ornate old-world interior makes for a classic cinema experience. This is where Rigensians head to see films from all around the globe. Elizabetes 61.
 728 11 05. Trolleybus 1, 3, 5, 7, 19, 21 or 24.

RETAIL THERAPY

Laima Did someone say chocolate? This Old Town location is just one of many places in Riga to get your sugar hit. Laima Chocolate is truly good stuff. Don't say we didn't warn you! Smilsu iela 16.

Livs Specialising in linen, and original Baltic jewellery in silver and bronze. Weaving demonstrations are frequently held in the shop.
 Kaleju iela 7. 722 90 10.

Mara Located inside the hotel Konventa Seta, this is where you can find both traditional souvenirs and Baltic amber jewellery.
 Kaleju iela 9/11.

Tine This is where you can find, well, practically any kind of souvenir you might desire. Spread over two floors is a wide selection of ceramics, amber, trinkets, linen, wool mittens and socks.
ⓐ Valnu iela 2.

Jekaba Kazarmas (St James' Barracks) What do you do with an old army barracks? Why not turn it into a chic collection of brand-name stores, boutiques and antique shops? Located at the edge of the Old Town. ⓐ Torna iela 4.

Basteja Pasaza A shopping centre so upmarket you might get a nosebleed just from window-shopping. Filled with the likes of Cerruti, Joop and others, it's no wonder this is a place selected for fashion shows on a regular basis. If shopping is not enough, you'll find a nice wine cellar and a beauty salon, too. ⓐ Basteja iela 16.

Valters un Rapa Large bookshop well-stocked with coffee-table books about Riga, stationery and calendars.
ⓐ Aspazijas bulvaris 24.

Japa Seta Need a map or guidebook? Look no further than this bookshop. Known for its excellent selection of both books and maps.
ⓐ Elizabetes iela 83/85.

Globuss A very good selection of English-language books can be found within this shop, along with a second-floor café where you can relax and read English-language newspapers. ⓐ Valnu iela 26.

Skarnu iela Right near St Peter's Church you'll find people hawking anything from knitwear to artwork – however, 'caveat emptor'.

TAKING A BREAK

Hesburger Finland's popular fast-food chain has reached the shores of Riga. Like its American counterpart, McDonald's, it offers a menu based on burgers, fries and sodas. ❸ Skunu 3. ❶ 750 03 09. ⏱ Daily 08.00–24.00.

I Love You Don't let the name dissuade you from entering. Inside you'll find dark wooden chairs, plush sofas, exposed brick walls and hardwood floors that create a cosy ambiance where you can put up your feet and snack on salads, sandwiches or even a cocktail. ❸ Aldaru iela 9. ❶ 722 53 04. ⏱ Daily from 10.00–24.00; Friday and Saturday 10.00–03.00.

John Lemon Cool. Bohemian. Hip. Comfy booths to drink, smoke or read a novel at almost any hour of the day. Sustenance for the unbearably hip includes casseroles, salads and soups. ❸ Peldu iela 21. ❶ 722 66 47. ⏱ Mon–Thur 10.00–02.00; Friday and Saturday 10.00–05.00; Sunday 12.00–24.00.

Olé No toreadors or bullfights in sight, just one of Riga's better buffets, featuring an astonishing range of cuisines from sweet and sour to aubergine Parmesan. ❸ Audeju iela 1. ❶ 722 95 63. ⏱ 07.30–17.00 Mon–Fri, closed Sat and Sun.

Petergailis Named after the golden rooster perched atop neighbouring St Peter's , this café serves hearty Baltic fare at a good price. An added bonus is the historic black-and-white photos adorning the walls that show Riga in its heyday (pre-Soviet occupation). ❸ Skarnu iela 25. ❶ 721 28 88. ⏱ Daily 11.00–23.00

AFTER DARK

Columbine A little bit of everything is what you can expect to find at this upmarket eatery. Entrees as diverse as tandoori or oysters on the half shell are just a sampling of what you can expect to find. One of the few restaurants in Riga that features a daily special. ⓐ Aspazijas bulv. 36/38 (Metropole). ⓣ 721 61 61. ⓛ Daily 12.00–23.00.

Hamlet Club Intimate venue for jazz concerts and impromptu theatre performances. Wonderfully spontaneous, and even if you can't understand the spoken language, you'll have no difficulty with the body language. ⓐ Jana seta iela 5. ⓣ 722 99 38.

Idalgo In the mood for a special wine? Step into this dark, medieval wine cellar and prepare to sample some of the best wines to be found in Riga. The food is not on a par with the wine selections, but the romantic atmosphere helps to compensate for any culinary deficiencies. ⓐ Teatra iela 12. ⓣ 722 18 29. ⓛ Daily 11.00–23.00.

Jautras Masas Start your night out on the town in this intimate little spot. A good place to try some of the lesser known Latvian beers, along with an appetiser. ⓐ Kaleju iela 9/11 (Konventa Seta). ⓣ 722 92 01. ⓛ Daily 10.00–22.00, 10.00–18.00 Sun.

Kreisais Pagrieziens A stylish club that draws both local and European artists such as Marija Naumova. Lots of 'unplugged' concerts are recorded here, so be prepared to be a hushed and respectful audience during a taping. ⓐ Kalku iela 11a. ⓣ 721 25 75. ⓕ 721 25 75. ⓛ Tues–Wed 20.00–01.00, Thur–Sat 20.00–05.00.

Lilze Jazz Bar New enough not to have acquired that lived-in feel but the menu is good and the main purpose for coming is to hear the live bands that perform every Tuesday, Thursday, Friday and Saturday. ⓐ Vecpilsetas iela 19. ⓣ 749 09 65 . ⓛ Daily 11.00–01.00.

Melnais Kakis (Black Cat) After most of the bars shut their doors it's time to head to the Black Cat for a good meal, some pinball, darts or a video game. Quirky, but anything after the bars are closed is destined to be unusual. ⓐ Meistaru iela 10/12. ⓣ 751 70 11. ⓛ Daily 09.00–07.00.

Mi6 If you ever dreamed of being James or Jane Bond, this is the place to while away an hour or two. Bond movies play on the TV, posters of Connery, Brosnan and even Stalin bedeck the walls. At heart, it's your basic Baltic booze establishment, but with a touch of fun. ⓐ Kaleju iela 52. ⓣ 722 76 11. ⓛ Daily 10.00–01.00, 10.00–4.30 Fri, 04.30–01.00 Sat, 16.00–02.00 Sun.

Paddy Whelan's Bright, lively and just Irish enough to make you think you could be in Dublin. If you want a quiet pint, head upstairs to the mellower Paddy Go Easy. ⓐ Grecinieku iela 4 (2nd floor). ⓣ 721 02 49. ⓛ Daily 15.00–24.00, 15.00–02.00 Fri–Sat.

Runcis (Tomcat) Totally Latvian from its beer and food to the regulars who frequent this bar. So relaxed you'll find the patrons playing chess and cards. ⓐ Jana seta iela 1. ⓣ 722 41 98. ⓛ Daily 12.00–02.00, 14.00–01.00 Sat–Sun.

▶ *Head for Paddy Whelan's for a taste of Ireland in Riga*

Vecmeita Ar Kaki (The Spinster and her Kitty) A friendly atmosphere and cheap specials. ❷ Maza Pils iela 1. ❶ 750 85 64. ⏺ Daily 11.00–23.00.

Outer Riga

East of the tangled streets of Old Riga rises New Riga, the two areas well defined by the city's old defensive moat, the Pilsetas Kanals (see page 64) or City Canal. Wide boulevards and park areas define the 19th-century influence, and the abundant art nouveau architecture adds the flavour of the wealthy early 20th century.

This part of Riga is filled with monuments and memorials to the recent turmoils that have affected this country. On Brivibas bulvaris stands the Freedom Monument, affectionately known as 'Milda', a striking liberty figure, crowned with three stars. This monument became a rallying point of the Latvian Independence movement in 1987. During the years of Soviet occupation a statue of Lenin, facing in the opposite direction, was erected only two blocks east of the monument. It has since been removed.

North of the Freedom Monument, red stone slabs stand as memorials to the dead of 20 January 1991, when Soviet troops stormed the Ministry of the Interior at nearby Raina bulvaris 6. This site is known locally as the Bastion Hill Memorial.

The impressive Fine Arts Museum lies at the northern end of the Esplanade park. The permanent collection features works of Russian and Latvian artists, and other artists are featured in temporary or travelling exhibitions. Once a planetarium during the Soviet occupation the Russian Orthodox Cathedral, at the southern end of the esplanade, has returned to its status as a church. In the same park you will also find a monument to Janis Rainis, Latvia's national poet, who some say would have been world-famous had he written his works in a less obscure language.

▶ *The Freedom Monument – Milda is Riga's lady liberty*

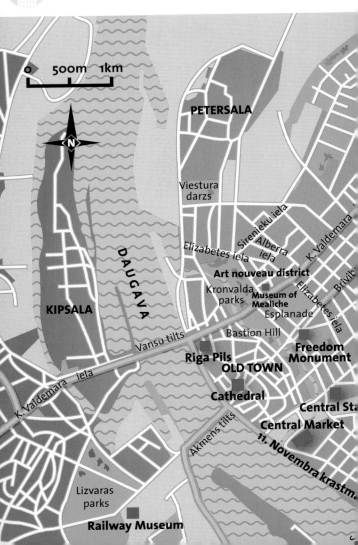

o 500m 1km

N

PETERSALA

Viestura
darzs

Sireneku iela
Alberra
iela
Elizabetes iela
K. Valdemara
Art nouveau district
Brivib
Kronvalda
parks
Museum of
Mealiche
Elizabetes iela
Esplanade
Bastion Hill

DAUGAVA

KIPSALA

Vansu tilts

Freedom
Monument

Riga Pils
OLD TOWN

K. Valdemara iela

Cathedral

Central Sta

Central Market

Akmens tilts

11. Novembra krastm

Lizvaras
parks

Railway Museum

GRIZINKALNS

1905
parks

Ziedondarzs

PURVCIEMS

Miera
darzs

St Vagonu
parks

Klusais
darzs

Most of suburban Riga is not much to write home about. Like all good urban sprawl, it's a mix of the good, the bad and the strip mall. One outstanding exception is Mezaparks (Forest Park). This area was once Riga's poshest residential district. Most of the construction took place prior to World War I and continued until the 1930s, and it includes examples of art nouveau, Romanticism and Rationalism.

SIGHTS & ATTRACTIONS

Bastion Hill Memorial

Five memorial stones in this central location are a haunting reminder of the Soviet crackdown in Riga in 1991. Five citizens were killed, some hit by stray bullets, as Soviet troops stormed a nearby Interior Ministry building.

Brivibas piemineklis (Freedom Monument)

This national shrine was unveiled in 1935. Designed by Karlis Zale, the friezes around the base of the structure depict Latvians singing, working and fighting for their freedom. The three stars in the maiden's crown depict the three historical regions of the country – Kurzeme, Vidzeme and Latgale. It is a tradition to place flowers at the base of the monument. During the Soviet occupation this act could mean a quick trip to Siberia. The honour guard changes every hour on the hour from 09.00 –18.00.

ⓐ Brivibas bulv. & Raina bulv. ⓦ Trolleybuses 1, 3, 7, 19 or 24.

Art nouveau district

The increasing prosperity of the late 19th century and early 20th

---

▶ *The Guards of the Motherland stare out from the Freedom Monument*

century resulted in an expansion of Riga beyond its central hub. This could not have happened at a more fortuitous time of design than that of the explosion of the art nouveau style.

The architectural style that developed in Austria and Germany, where it was known as *Jugendstil*, has left its imprint on cities from Paris to St Petersburg. Buildings are characterised by their decorations: floral patterns, human faces and mythical figures. This was more than just a fashion trend: art nouveau infiltrated almost all aspects of life at that time. Evidence of its influence could be found on everything from buildings to tableware, paintings to cocktail shakers. At the time this style was becoming popular, Riga was a very important port in the Russian empire, with a booming economy, growing population and lots of money to spend. The result was such that more than 40 per cent of the buildings in Riga have been designed in the style of art nouveau.

Most of Riga's art nouveau treasures escaped the devastation of World War II and the majority of buildings remained mainly untouched. Since then the economy has had a more debilitating effect. Property nationalised by the Communists has now been returned to pre-1940 owners. However, most of them don't have the resources to restore the houses to their former glory, and they sit with cracked facades and chipped paintwork. A few of the apartment buildings have been restored and sold, mostly to foreign businessmen, who seem to be the only ones who can afford these new luxuries.

Take a walking tour of the best of the art nouveau buildings. Start at the north corner of the Esplanade and go west on Elizabetes iela. You will see many buildings designed by Eisenstein.

▶ *In Riga you can see art nouveau at its most theatrical*

Continue along Elizabetes, turn right on Strelnieku iela and then turn right again on Alberta iela. Nymphs and mythical figures grace the facades of everyday buildings. Floral motifs bloom on the fronts of apartment buildings and bay windows sprout like weeds. No wonder the utilitarian architecture of the Soviet era stands out in stark comparison.

Fire-fighting Museum of Latvia
An art nouveau style firehouse? Yes, indeed. This museum is housed in a former fire station built in that classic style. Inside you'll find collections featuring equipment, flags, uniforms and photographs outlining the history of fire-fighting from the 19th century until today.

ⓐ Hanzas iela 5. ☎ 733 13 34. ⌚ 11.00–17.00. Closed Mon and Tues.

Stradinsh Museum of Medicine

Latvia's famous Dr Paul Stradins collected antique, tribal and unusual cures and medicines for more than 30 years. This collection has been assembled into one of the largest museums of medicine in the world. Quirky, and sometimes a little bit morbid, this museum will definitely intrigue.

ⓐ Antonijas iela 1. ⓣ 733 42 23. ⓛ 11.00–17.00. Closed Sun–Mon & last Fri of every month. Ⓝ Trolleybus 1, 19 or 24.

Centraltirgus (Central Market)

At the end of its construction in 1930, Riga's Central Market was one of the largest and most modern marketplaces in Europe. The market was built with five Zeppelin hangars from World War I. Four of these

---

ⓥ *The airships have been replaced by stalls in Riga's central market*

buildings still function as meat, fish, produce and dairy markets. The atmosphere bustles with activity, and although you might find a few merchants open to haggling, the majority are reluctant to do so.

🅐 Centraltirgus iela, near the central railway station.

🕐 Tues–Sat 08.00–17.00, Sun–Mon 08.00–16.00.

Museum of Nature

This museum of natural history is one of the oldest museums in the country, dating back to 1846. The collections, spread over four floors, include a variety of fossils, plants, animals and some interactive exhibits.

🅐 Kr. Barona iela 4. 📞 722 60 78. 🕐 10.00–17.00, Thur 12.00–19.00, closed Mon–Tues.

KGB Victims' Memorial

You would hardly guess that the unassuming and rusting doors of this memorial, wedged between a coffee shop, a cocktail bar, a striptease club and a police station, were once the very gates of misery. The text on the left side sums it up neatly: 'During the Soviet occupation the state security agency, the KGB, imprisoned, tortured, killed and morally humiliated its victims in this building.'

🅐 Strelnieku laukums 1. 📞 721 27 15.

State Museum of Art

A fine and varied collection of Latvian and Russian art that includes the work of painters such a V. Purvitis, Janis Rozentals, Nikolain Rerih and I. Aivazovsky.

🅐 Kr. Valdemara iela 10a. 📞 732 44 61. 🌐 www.vmml.v.

🕐 11.00–17.00. Closed Tues. 🚎 Trolleybus 5.

Latvian Photography Museum

See how photography has developed from the primitive techniques of the 19th century to the digital era of the new millennium. Transparencies, negatives, photographic equipment and outstanding photos are all a part of this intriguing collection.
ⓐ Marstula iela 8 (entrance from Alksnaja iela). ❶ 722 72 31.
🕒 Wed, Thur 13.00–19.00, Fri, Sat 11.00–17.00, Sun 11.00–15.00. Closed Mon and Tues.

Open-air Ethnographic Museum

Over 100 hectares (200 acres) of life as it used to be during a more pastoral period in Latvia's history. Farmsteads, windmills, churches and fishing villages have been relocated to this site and restored for posterity. You can watch craftsmen ply their trades, see costumed 'villagers' and partake of Latvian food and drink in the tavern.
ⓐ Brivibas gatve 440. ❶ 799 45 15. 🕒 Daily 10.00–17.00. Admission charge.

Motor Museum

You don't have to be a motorhead or a youngster to appreciate the assembled collection of automobiles from bygone days. If you ever wondered what Stalin drove, or yearned to see the car Breshnev crashed on a joy ride, this is the place. There is also an exhibit of antique motorbikes on site.
ⓐ Eizensteina iela 6. ❶ 709 71 70. 🕒 Tue-Sun 10.00–18.00, Mon 10.00–15.00.

Mezaparks (Forest Park)

This area was once Riga's poshest residential district. Most of the construction took place prior to World War I and continued until the

1930s. Architecture buffs can admire the various styles, including art nouveau, Romanticism and Rationalism.

Riga Zoo
Set amid the hilly pines of Mezaparks, the zoo has a substantial collection of mammals, including eight bears from brown to polar. You'll also find traditional zoo favourites such as zebras and camels.
📍 Meza Prospekts 1. ☎ 751 86 89. 🕐 Daily 10.00–18.00. Admission charge 🚌 Tram 11 from Kr. Barona iela: Zoologiskais darz stop.

CULTURE

Daile (Baltic Cinema) Classics and previously run Hollywood blockbusters are the staples at this two-screen theatre.
📍 Kr. Barona iela 31. ☎ 728 28 54. 🚌 Tram 3 or 6; trolleybus 1, 4, 5, 7, 13, 14 or 17.

Gamblings Bridge-playing fiends of Riga, including a lot of Latvia's top bridge masters, head to this spot. A card club and restaurant, this is where people come to socialise and improve their game.
📍 Brivibas iela 156. 🕐 12.00–24.00.

K. Suns This renovated theatre with soothing plush seating is almost exclusively dedicated to showing arty or European variety films. 📍 Elizabetes iela 83–85. ☎ 728 54 11. 🚌 Trolleybus 1, 3, 5, 7, 19, 21 or 24.

Lido Slivotava
The active life is certainly a part of Riga's culture, so strap on a pair of skates and join the throng at this rink. After you've worked up an

appetite have a snack or a beer before pressing on. ⓐ Krasta 76.
ⓣ 750 44 20. ⓛ Daily: 10.00–23.00. ⓝ Tram 3, 7 or 9.

Puppet Theatre

You have to love a theatre that allows you to adjust the height of
your seat, so that even the smallest patron can get a good view of
the stage. ⓐ Kr. Barona iela 16/18. ⓣ 728 54 18. ⓝ Tram 1, 3 or 6;
trolleybus 3, 4, 17, 19 or 24.

Riga Once called the Splendid Palace, the ornate old-world interior
of this theatre makes for a classic cinema experience. This is where
Rigensians head to see films from all around the globe.
ⓐ Elizabetes iela 61. ⓣ 728 11 05. ⓝ Trolleybus 1, 3, 5, 7, 19, 21 or 24.

Riga Circus At nearly a century old, the Riga Circus is the only
permanent circus in the Baltics. The shows run from mid-October
until April, with special productions during both Christmas and
Easter. Not your usual circus, the acts include some performing pigs
and not-so-performing cats. ⓐ Merkela 4. ⓣ 721 32 79.

RETAIL THERAPY

Barona Centrs Another large mall (40 stores) smack in the middle of
town. ⓐ Kr. Barona iela 46. ⓣ 750 84 03. ⓛ daily, 10.00–20.00.

Central Market Adjacent to the rail station, these five large
buildings that once stored Zeppelins are the place to find almost
anything. ⓐ Pragas 1 (see pages 90–92).

Domina Polished, upmarket and oozing with city chic. Fashion,

Italian restaurants, coffee shops and a Maxima hypermarket.
⊕ Ierku 4. ⊚ Trolleybus 18 or 23 from Caka across the bridge. Domina
is on your left. ⊕ 10.00 – 20.00.

Mols Similar to Centrs (see pages 24–25), but in the suburbs. There
are an excellent sushi bar and some really good coffee shops to keep
you fortified while shopping till you drop. ⊕ Krasta 4. ⊚ Tram 7 or 9:
Maza Kaina stop. Then walk down Toma iela or take one of the free
mini-buses marked 'Mols' from the rail station. ⊕ 10.00–20.00.

Origo Great big shopping centre right next to the train station and
filled with everything, including fashion outlets and services such as
dry cleaning. ⊕ Stacijas laukums 2.

Palazzo Italia Gorgeous clothes and all the accessories to go with
them. Be prepared to take out a second mortgage for a complete
outfit. ⊕ Kr. Barona iela 2. ⊕ 707 09 30. ⊕ Daily, 10.45–19.45.

Stockmann's Finland's number-one department store has finally
opened its doors in Riga. Four floors of fashion and everything for your
home. And, if that's not enough, there's a supermarket for picnic fixings
and a delicatessen if you don't 'cook'. This is also a great place to stock
up on cosmetics. ⊕ Janvara 13. ⊕ Daily, 09.00–22.00.

TAKING A BREAK

Blinoff If it is a crêpe you crave, head for Blinoff. The Russian-style
pancakes are stuffed with potato, apples, vegetables, chicken, pork
or beef, and topped with sour cream or jam. ⊕ Brivibas bulv. 30.
⊕ Mon–Fri 09.00–2200, Sat–Sun 10.00–22.00.

Cetri Veji Good food at cheap prices served up in an atmosphere of American 1950s kitsch and sprinkled with a dash of other antiques.
🅐 Bruninieku 35. ☎ 731 34 63. 🕒 Mon–Sat 10.30–23.00. Closed Sun.

Chicko Chicken Bright, modern and tasty. The menu is simple: fried chicken, beer and brownies all ready to takeaway. Be patient with the slow service; the food is worth the wait and very reasonably priced. 🅐 Kr. Barona iela 44. ☎ 800 06 06.
🕒 Mon–Thur 10.00–02.00, Fri–Sat 10.00–03.00, Sun 10.00–24.00.

David's Cappuccino Bar Polished place to sip a truly good coffee and indulge yourself with a pastry or cake.
🅐 Dzirnavu 113 (Upiza pasaza). ☎ 728 16 49. 🕒 daily 09.00–21.00, Sat–Sun 10.00–21.00.

Double Coffee Try and imagine a Starbucks with cocktails and sushi as well as coffee, tea and chocolate. Something for everyone.
🅐 Terbatas 5; 🆆 www.doublecoffee.com 🕒 24 hours a day.

Fazer Café Tucked into the fourth floor of Stockmann's department store is a refreshing restaurant with a large buffet, salad bar and a pancake counter. Sustenance to keep on shopping.
🅐 Stockmann's, Janvara 8. 🕒 Daily 09.00–22.00.

Green Hall This greenhouse restaurant is nearly so overgrown with plants you may wish you had brought a machete to help you hack your way to one of the best buffets in Riga. Low prices, but after 18.00 you'll have to pay a cover charge of 0.10L just to sip a coffee.
🅐 Gertrudes 33/35 (entrance from Martas). ☎ 729 23 86.
🕒 Mon–Thur 11.00–19.00, Fri 11.00–20.00, closed Sat–Sun.

Lauvas Nams Shashlik and other grilled meats cooked under the harsh glare of neon lights. The meals are good, cheap and available around the clock. ⓐ Brivibas iela 82. ① 729 76 45. ◐ Daily, 24hrs.

Panna Pancakes Pancakes and more pancakes. What else would you expect from a restaurant decked out as a large frying pan with huge wooden spoons? Be sure to try the fried banana ones. ⓐ Marijas 23. ① 728 53 97. ◐ Mon–Fri 09.00–21.00, Sat–Sun 11.00–20.00.

Pizza Lulu New York-style (cheesy and thin-crusted) pizza by the slice or an entire pie served in a cosy brick-walled atmosphere. ⓐ Gertrudes 27. ① 800 58 58. Ⓦ www.lulu.lv

AFTER DARK

Restaurants
Barons Sports Bar This is the place to eat, drink and watch sports. Covering three floors, there are enough TVs, including a huge screen in the back hall, to keep any sports enthusiast happy for hours. ⓐ Kr. Barona iela 108. ① 729 97 07. Ⓦ www.barons.lv ◐ Mon–Thur 11.00–23.00, Fri–Sat 11.00–01.00.

Bellevue Located on the West Bank of the River, atop the 11th floor of the hotel, you'll find one of Riga's premier restaurants. Seafood delicacies are a speciality and the desserts are so decadent you'll be tempted to kidnap the pastry cook. ⓐ Slokas 1, Maritim Park Hotel. ① 706 90 00. ◐ Daily 18.00–23.00.

◗ *There are clubs all over the city including La Rocca, one of the largest*

Bergs Flambéed scallops wrapped in prosciutto with tomato and papaya salsa is just one entrée that will make your taste buds cry out for more. The decor is straight out of *Architectural Digest* and the bill at the end of the evening may have you applying for a second mortgage, but the meal will be memorable. ⓐ Elizabetes iela 83/85. ⓣ 777 09 49. ⓦ www.hotelbergs.lv . ⓛ daily 12.00–24.00.

Piramida The local press refers to Piramida as 'the little Louvre' because of the glass structure that houses this elegant restaurant. Buffets are offered at both breakfast and lunch. ⓐ Reimersa 1 (Park Hotel Ridzene). ⓣ 732 44 33. ⓛ Daily 07.00–23.30.

Entertainment
Bites Bluzs Klubs Just the way a blues club should be – dark, moody, serving good food and good beer. The entertainment is also good, sometimes from as far away as America. ⓐ Dzirnavu 34a. ⓣ 733 31 25. ⓛ Mon–Thur 12.00–01.00, Fri–Sat 12.00–02.00.

La Rocca You won't find a larger, livelier or noisier nightclub in all of Riga, possibly the Baltics. This converted theatre specialises in 'techno' music and the clientele is mostly clad in spandex. Surprisingly, the drinks are very cheap. ⓐ Brivibas iela 96. ⓣ 750 60 30. ⓛ Thur–Sat 22.00–09.00, Sun 22.00–06.00. Cover charge

Sarkans There is nightlife indeed outside of the Old Town! Join the throng of young and not-so-young party animals at the long bar, disco dance floor or the lounge. ⓐ Stabu 10. ⓣ 727 22 86. ⓛ Mon–Thur 10.00–24.00, Fri 10.00–04.00, Sat–Sun 12.00–24.00.

ⓞ *Sigulda's public buildings and parks are now well tended*

OUT OF TOWN
trips

Jurmala

Once the seaside playground of Tsarist nobles, this area became the summer getaway for the wealthy Riga city dweller by the 1920s. No expense was spared in creating beautiful summer homes by the sea, and you'll see influences of art nouveau, romanticism and classical architecture. What makes this art nouveau area different from that of Riga's? Here the construction was done in wood. The list of architectural monuments has over 400 entries!

Shortly after the end of World War II, Jurmala became the preferred choice of Soviet citizens to take their holiday. Today the beaches and pine forests are simply teeming with people on weekends and holidays. The long stretches of beach and sand dunes interspersed with fragrant stands of pine make a delightful location

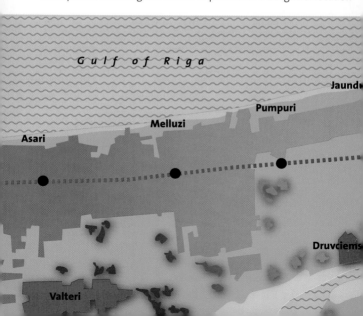

Gulf of Riga

Jaund

Pumpuri

Melluzi

Asari

Druvciems

Valteri

to while away a day or two. Jurmala is the combined name for the string of small towns and resorts that stretch almost 20 km (12.5 miles) along the coast west of Riga. But a few are readily reached by train. Starting from the eastern end you can visit Lielupe, Bulduri, Majori and Valteri. Most of the action seems to be centred around the town of Majori. In all there are 15 villages that comprise 'Jurmala' and in 1959 they were united, mostly for administrative purposes.

At one time the beaches of the Baltic were so polluted you had to be extremely careful about swimming. However, those at Majori and Bulduri have recently been awarded the coveted 'Blue Flag', an award based on water quality, environmental management, safety and a very important criterion – toilet facilities.

Aside from beach activities you'll find plenty to do at Latvia's seaside. Walking the beaches, dunes and forests is reason enough to

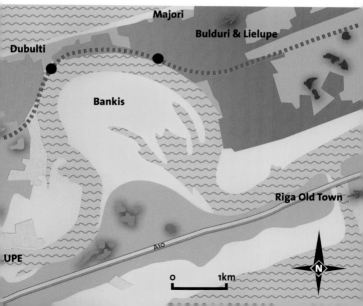

visit. And the nightlife is plentiful with restaurants, nightclubs, cabarets and casinos.

Jurmala is only a short train ride of about 40 minutes from Riga's Central Station and the service is very frequent. If you prefer to drive, you'll soon discover that the road to Jurmala is possibly the best stretch of highway in the entire country; of course it's only about 15 km. Be prepared– there is a toll for using this bit of highway.

Jurmala Spa and Tourism Information Centre
ⓐ Jomas iela 42, Majori, Jurmala, ⓣ 776 34 93.
ⓦ www.jurmalatour.lv

ⓞ *One of Jurmala's quiet beaches, this one is at Majori*

SIGHTS & ATTRACTIONS

The primary reason to pry yourself away from the city is to be in the great outdoors! Yes, there are museums and theatres aplenty, but kick off your shoes, grab a sandwich, slap on some sunscreen and be at one with the sea.

Jurmala Open-air Museum

Created to portray the life of Latvian fishermen in the late 19th and early 20th centuries, this collection is filled with wooden homes, anchors, nets, ropes and antique boats. Located not far from where the Lielupe River flows into the Gulf of Riga, a little way out of town.
ⓐ Tiklu iela 1a, Lielupe. ⓣ 774 49 09. ⓛ 10.00–18.00. Closed Mon. ⓝ Bus 1.

Dubulti Luteragu Baznica

This beautiful church was constructed during the time of the art nouveau rage in 1909. Like most Lutheran churches, the interior is simple, but the fantastic spire is very impressive. ⓐ Baznica iela 13, Dubulti.

Seno Spekratu Izstade (Antique Car Exhibition)

Spend an afternoon in this exhibition of classic cars. Lincolns, Mercedes and BMWs are all garaged together, along with some motorcycles (some with sidecars) from days gone by. ⓐ Turaida iela 11, Dzintari ⓣ 926 33 29. ⓛ 11.00–18.00. Donation requested.

Jurmalas Globe

If you don't have a clue where in the world you are, then this is a good place to pin it down. Latvia's largest globe was renovated in 2003, so with its spiffy new coat of paint it makes a great photo opportunity. ⓐ Crossing of Turaidas iela and Jomas iela, between Dzintari and Majori.

CULTURE

Dzintari Concert Hall Built in 1936, this sumptuous concert hall is a very popular place for concerts, both indoors and outside in the gardens. ⓐ Turaidas iela 1, Dzintari. ⓣ 776 20 05. ⓦ www.dzk.lv

RETAIL THERAPY

Like all good beach destinations, this is not where you come to do any serious shopping. The main shops can be found on Jomas iela,

and the stretch between Dubulti and Dzintari has the chic-est
selection. Elsewhere it's mostly buckets and spades, floating devices,
cheap beach towels and postcards.

TAKING A BREAK/AFTER DARK

Datorklubs An excellent internet café. You may have to fight your
way through hordes of teenagers glued to computer screens to
check your email, but the staff are very helpful and there's also a
printer and scanner available. ⓐ Jomas iela 62, Majori. ☏ 781 14 11.

Bistro Princites £ Inexpensive Latvian fast food only a stone's throw
from the beach. ⓐ Juras iela 46, Majori. ☏ 942 16 97. ◷ Daily
11.00–20.00.

Klondika Tex-Mex £–££ This popular chain of restaurants/gambling
halls has made its way to the seashore. What money you'll save on the
almost authentic cuisine you may just lose in the slot machines.
ⓐ Talsu soseja 31, Kauguri. ☏ 774 06 88. ◷ Daily 09.00–07.00.

Caviar Club £££ Want great gourmet dining and a view of the sea?
Caviar Club is the experience you are seeking. Goose liver paté, sea
bass, swordfish, and, of course, the house speciality caviar with
potato pancakes, blini or salmon. ⓐ Baltic Beach Club Hotel, Juras
iela 23/25, Majori. ☏ 771 14 00. ◷ Daily 07.00–02.00.

ACCOMMODATION

Rakstnieju Names £ A charming house with large rooms and plenty
of natural light streaming in through the windows. Not much in the

way of standard amenities, this lodging is meant for writers seeking a retreat from modern-day distractions.
ⓐ Akas iela 4, Dubuti. ☎ 776 99 65.

Juras Banga ££ Charming, shabby-chic decor with outrageous colour schemes, but someone really should tell them that pink and aquamarine really don't blend all that well. However, the rooms, although small, have TV, refrigerator and clean bathrooms. Given the price (cheap), and its location right next to the beach, it's hard to complain. ⓐ Juras iela 30, Majori. ☎ 776 23 92. ☎ 776 15 38.

Majori ££ If finding your way back to the hotel has ever been a problem then you'll appreciate that the green tower of this art nouveau building is visible from all over the town. The rooms are not large, but they are pleasant and have private bath, cable TV and telephone. Suites feature a refrigerator and stereo.
ⓐ Jomas iela 29, Majori.

Lielupe ££–£££ This super-size hotel offers both business and economy-class accommodation. Business rooms are large with all sorts of modern conveniences such as satellite TV, mini bar, phone and an in-room safe. The economy rooms are clean, comfortable and a very good deal. The hotel offers indoor and outdoor swimming pools, tennis courts, a spa, children's room, bicycle rental and a 10th-floor restaurant with the best views in town.
ⓐ Bulduri iela 64/68, Bulduri. ☎ 775 27 55. ☎ 775 26 94.

Pegasa Pils ££–£££ This turn-of-the-20th century art nouveau masterpiece has been thoroughly renovated and updated. The rooms are decorated in warm colours with comfortable

furniture and offer satellite TV, telephone, mini-bar, and private balcony. A restaurant and sauna are also available.
📍 Juras iela 60, Majori. ☎ 776 11 49. 📠 776 11 69.

Alve £££ A pleasing small hotel, only ten rooms, that places an emphasis on health programmes. The spa offers some serious treatments such as 'therapeutic fasting' and 'body cleansing' at an additional cost. 📍 Jomas iela 88a, Majori. ☎ 779 59 71.
📠 779 59 72.

Kursi £££ These contemporary-design brick and stucco cottages are quite unlike anything else in the area. Almost all the doubles and suites are set on two floors, with a small kitchen, living room, private bath, satellite TV and telephone. If you feel like splurging, ask for the suite with the bar and fireplace. Breakfast is not included.
📍 Dubulti iela 30, Dubulti. ☎ 777 16 06. 📠 777 16 05.

Motel Mango £££ A modern motel with multiple personalities. Each room is decorated differently, some with oddly ornate furniture and one with a safe hidden behind a painting á la James Bond. All the rooms feature telephone, satellite TV and a full bath with bathtub. A small pool, sauna, billiard room and a zebra-striped café complete the unusual ambience.
📍 Bulduri prospekts 30, Bulduri. ☎ 775 24 11. 📠 776 22 99.

Baltic Beach Club Hotel £££–£££+ Located right on the beach of the Gulf of Riga. The hotel features a swimming pool, restaurant and fitness centre with sauna and steam bath. The spa is state-of-the-art and the on-site restaurant is one of the best in the area. 📍 Juras iela 23/25, Majori. ☎ 777 14 00. 📠 777 14 10. 🌐 www.balticbeach.lv

Eastern Latvia

A day trip east of Riga will introduce you to some of the loveliest parts of Latvia. If you've had all you want of the medieval architecture, hustle and bustle of city life in Riga then it must be time to grab a train and head for the outdoor life. Be sure to have extra cards for your digital camera because you're going to use a lot of pixels in this part of the country.

The valley of the Gauja River, between the towns of Valmiera and Sigulda, is possibly the most picturesque area of Latvia. It is also one of the most historic. The river has cut its winding path through the sandstone, leaving rocky cliffs and forested banks.

In 1207, about the same time as Riga was being founded, the area was split between the Knights of the Sword (later the Livonian Order – a German crusading order allied to the Teutonic Knights) who got the south bank of the river, and the Archbishop of Riga, who claimed the north bank. The area remained split between various invading factions for centuries. Although the country is now united, the residents on either side of the river still speak distinctly different dialects.

The area reminded the Germans so much of central Europe that they referred to it as Livonian Switzerland, even though the mountains are barely 100m (330ft) high.

Starting at Sigulda, only 50 km (31 miles) east of Riga, this destination is easily reached by train, bus or automobile. The area has been set aside as the Gaujas National Park in order to save its great natural beauty. Besides many caves, hiking trails and nature paths, the area is laced with castles, palaces and churches. The park is perfect for canoeing, hiking and just kicking back.

Cêsis, a short 90 km (56 miles) from Riga, is easily reached by car

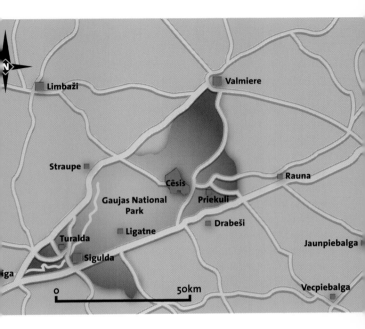

or public transport. There is an hourly bus service between Riga and Cesis, and four trains a day, also stopping at Sigulda. All the sights of the town centre are within a short distance of each other, making for a compact sightseeing experience.

SIGHTS & ATTRACTIONS

SIGULDA

Sigulda is the closest entry point to the area. Following the restoration of Latvia's independence, Sigulda experienced a resurgence in the preservation of public buildings and parks, and, more importantly, in the services offered to tourists. Sigulda is also the site of the Latvian bobsleigh run (see pages 115–116, 123).

In the spring a town festival is held around the time of the cherry trees blossoming, in summer an open-air Opera Festival takes place in the castle ruins, autumn is the time to watch the glorious colours of the trees, while winter is the season for skiing and bobsleigh racing.

Sigulda Castle

Built by German crusaders between 1207 and 1226, the castle was the first stone fortification to be constructed outside the city of Riga by foreign invaders. It was destroyed during the Great Northern War (1700–21). The remaining ruins, including the towering stone gate and the abandoned Gothic cathedral, have been partially restored, and an outdoor theatre has been built nearby for summer concerts. Adjacent to the ruins is the Sigulda New Castle, a manor house built during the late 19th century that now serves as the home of the town council. ⓐ Pils 16, Sigulda.

Turaida Castle

Once used as a stronghold of the Crusaders, Turaida Castle was built in 1214 by Riga's archbishop Albert. Today this museum is the largest protected cultural monument in the country. It is filled with artefacts dating from the 11th century and outlines the history of the now extinct Liv tribes who once lived in the surrounding hills. Restoration was done with new materials, so the castle lacks the

---

▶ *Archbishop Albert's version of the leaning tower, at Turaida Castle*

truly authentic feel of antiquity. Climb to the top of the tower to gaze upon a splendid panorama of Gauja Valley. ⓐ Turaidas iela 10, Sigulda. ⓣ 29 71 797. ⓛ 10.00–18.00.

Turaida Rose's Grave

The grave of an orphan beauty, the 'Rose of Turaida' (1601–20), lies at the foot of an ancient linden tree just outside the castle and church. Legend has it that a little girl named Maija was discovered by one of the castle staff after a fierce battle. He adopted the girl and raised her. Maija grew up in the castle grounds and eventually came to work there, where she fell in love with another commoner who worked in the gardens. Unfortunately, the beautiful young girl attracted the attention of a Polish soldier who asked for her hand in marriage. She refused and was kidnapped and taken to Gutman's cave. Here, the brave Maija chose death before submitting to the soldier. Today, newlyweds visit her grave on their wedding day and lay flowers at her grave in the hope of experiencing the same eternal love and fidelity she demonstrated to her beloved, but with the expectations of better results.

Gutman's Cave

This is the largest cave in the Baltic area at 19.8m deep, 12m wide and 10m high (64 x 40 x 33 ft). Legend has it that a Liv warrior ordered that his beautiful, but cheating, wife be entombed in the wall of a local cliff. The woman's tears turned into a clear stream of water, which eventually carved the massive cave out of the wall of rock. ⓐ 50 m (150 ft) off Turaidas iela, Sigulda.

Krimulda Palace

This yellow neo-classical building was once the seat of an

aristocratic German family, but it now serves as a sanatorium and is closed to the public. However, the grounds are open, and worth a visit. Nearby are the ruins of Krimulda Castle. Built in the 13th century, it overlooks the valley.

🄰 Mednicka iela 3, Sigulda.

Peter's Cave

This is a narrow cave in a sandstone wall along the embankment of the Vejupe river. The cave is only 6.5m (20ft) long and 5.3m (17 ft) high. The story of the cave is that, during Swedish rule in the 17th century, a farmer named Peter hid in the cave in order to escape being drafted into the army. Another legend claims that a local clergyman hid here and christened several children. Today, convenient steps lead to the cave for your exploration.

Dainu Kains (Folk Song Hill)

Stroll among the little stone people on Folk Song Hill. The statues reflect the various characters and aspects of Latvian folklore.

🄰 Next to Turaida Castle.

Gauja Valley Cable Car

Take in the gorgeous Gauja Valley and the Turaida Castle from a cable car as it crosses from one side of the river to the other. The Krimulda Castle ruins are directly to your right when you step out on the north side of the river.

🄰 Porku 14. ☏ 797 25 31. ☀ Daily 07.25–21.30.

Bobsleigh Track

The giant run of the national bobsleigh track was built by Yugoslavian experts in 1981. To get there, walk a few hundred metres

from the station along the train tracks in the direction of Riga. You won't be able to miss it (see page 123).

CESIS

Cesis draws both local and foreign tourists to this pastoral region, which has remained virtually untouched despite the two world wars. Cesis was founded in 1207 with the construction of a stone castle by German knights. It served as the headquarters for the Livonian Order until the 16th century. A city sprang up around the castle and grew so prosperous that it became a member of the Hanseatic League. Cesis also became the only Latvian city apart from Riga that had a mint for coining money, another testament to its prosperity.

Unfortunately Cesis fell victim to the wars and plagues of the 17th and 18th centuries and only began to recover in the 19th century when it was finally linked by road and rail to Riga.

All the sights of the town centre are within a short distance of each other, making for a compact sightseeing experience. Cesis is only 35 km up the road from Sigulda.

Castle of the Livonian Order

Latvia's most impressive and best preserved complex of castle ruins and the most popular site in Cesis. Some of the original castle of 1207 remains. The castle was expanded under the Livonian Order and the Swedes, but destroyed in 1703 by the Russians. An annexe added in the 18th century holds the Museum of History and Art.
ⓐ Pils laukums 11. ❶ 412 26 15. ❶ Tues–Sun 10.00–18.00. Admission charge.

---

❶ *Cesis boasts the best castle ruins in Latvia*

Museum of History and Art

The exhibits trace Latvian history from prehistoric times to the Latvian War of Liberation. The Lademacher Tower has an extensive view of Cesis and its environs.

St John's Church

Built in the late 13th century, this is now largest church of eastern Latvia, a testament to the wealth of the citizens in this flourishing area. It contains the tombs of several masters of the Livonian order.
ⓐ Skolas iela 8, Cesis. ⓣ 412 44 88.

The Cesis Victory Monument

The city's pride and joy, this monument is dedicated to those who fell in the cause of Latvian freedom at the Battles of Cesis in 1919. Erected in the 1920s, it was demolished by the Soviets in the 1950s, but reconstructed in the 1990s.
ⓐ Vienibas laukums, Cesis.

Rose Square

This has been the central square of Cesis since the mid-13th century. Over the centuries it has also become known as Market Square.

Cesis New Castle

The former residence of the owner of Cesis Castle Manor. Built in the late 18th century, it is on the site of the gate defences of the old castle. ⓐ Pils laukums 9, Cesis. ⓣ 412 26 15.

GAUJAS NATIONAL PARK

The Gauja River carves its way through about 40 km (25 miles) of hills of Devonian sandstone, as it winds its way from Valmiera to

Sigulda, leaving behind a surrealistic tangle of carved hills and forest-covered banks. Established in 1973 specifically to protect the indigenous flora and fauna, this park is simply the most beautiful in all of Latvia. Scattered through it are nature trails, sites to view various animals, hiking trails and viewing areas with steps and platforms from which you can see the area's ancient monuments and landscapes.

The river is excellent for canoeing, and paddling down the river is a good way to see the scenery. It is possible to rent canoes and rowing boats, guided or unguided, in Sigulda, Cesis and Valmiera.

Rauna Castle ruins

Begun in 1262 by the order of the Archbishop, this building was one of his main residences. ⓐ Rauna Parish.

Veselava Manor

This manor home was constructed in the 1840s, and was built to resemble a fortified medieval castle. The two-storey mansion of masonry is u-shaped and lies on an isolated oval plot of land, surrounded on all sides by a moat, which is almost completely dry at the present time. Tour the house and grounds and hear the legends of the Veselava family related by a guide. ⓐ Viesturi, Veselava Parish. ⓣ 419 22 32.

Araisi Lake Fortress

This is a reconstruction of an ancient Latgallian residential site of the 9th century. It is based on the building remains and artefacts discovered in excavations, and it is the Baltic's first open-air museum.

ⓐ Drabesi Parish. ⓣ 419 72 88.

Lielstraupe Castle

This castle was originally built in the Romanesque style of the 13th century. From the inner courtyard of cobblestones you can view all of the buildings and the gateway leading to the church and the park. ⊖ Straupe Parish.

Velna Cave

Legend has it that the Devil himself carved this cave into the wall when he was suddenly surprised by the sunlight appearing above the ground. A small cave at only 19m deep, 7m wide and 4.7m high, it can be seen from the left bank of the Gauja River.

Viktor's Cave

This is the only man-made cave in the region. Apparently, a baronial gardener, Viktor, carved the cave into the sandstone as a present for his bride, Maija. The woman could then sit in the cave and watch her loving husband paddle across the river to reach her side.

Wild Horse Pasture

This is Europe's most northerly enclosure for wild horses. Nine wild horses have been living in a natural habitat of 20 hectares since 2002. ⊖ Jaun-levinas, Rauna Parish. ⊕ 949 51 46.

Zvarte Rock

One of the most picturesque Devonian rock formations in the region. So good, you won't even mind the small admission fee. ⊖ Left Bank of the Amata. ⊕ 933 54 46.

▶ *The dramatic entrance to Gutman's cave, the largest in the Baltics*

OTHER EASTERN LATVIA SIGHTS

Ungurmuiza Manor

This unique example of 18th-century baroque wooden architecture is open to visitors. Stroll the grounds, take tea in the teahouse and admire the well-preserved murals on the interior walls.

ⓐ Rasikums Parish. **ⓣ** 415 82 23.

Janaskola

Emil Darzin's memorial museum tells the story of the composer's life and works. It is an excellent opportunity to listen to *The Melancholy Waltz* and other pieces by a composer who deserves to be better known outside his native country.

ⓐ Jaunpiebalga Parish. **ⓣ** 410 03 51.

Kaina Kaibeni

The memorial museum to the Kaudzite brothers, famous Latvian writers is Latvia's oldest museum and is attractive to visitors largely because of its unusual authenticity.

ⓐ Vecpiebalga Parish. **ⓣ** 416 82 16.

Saulrieti

This is the memorial museum of Karlis Skalbe, Latvia's best-loved poet and storyteller. It was established at the poet's summerhouse on Inceni Hill. The house tucks harmoniously into the hilly landscape and the balcony affords a view of Lake Alauksts.

ⓐ Vecpiebalga Parish. **ⓣ** 416 45 42.

ACTIVE LIFE

Bobsleigh track

Be bold! Take a ride in a summer or winter bobsleigh on the giant run. Although speeds during competitions can reach 125km/h 78 mph, your trip will be toned down a little.

ⓐ Sveices 13, Sigulda. **ⓣ** 797 38 13. **ⓕ** 797 20 26. **ⓛ** Sat–Sun 12.00–17.00.

Bungee jumping

Can't get enough blood-rushing-to-your-head experiences? Try the bungee jump from a cable car at a height of 43m (142 ft) over the Gauja River. It's best to call ahead for reservations.

ⓐ Poruka 14, Sigulda. **ⓣ** 644 06 60. **ⓛ** Sat and Sun from 18.30.

Off-road go-carts

Rent off-road mini-buggies and take a cruise over a private parcel of land in the countryside. Bumpy, fun and good for the motorheads among you.

ⓐ 300m beyond Sigulda on the Vidzeme Highway. **ⓣ** 927 76 47 4.

Turaidas Stallis

Take time for a more gentle activity with a pony ride or a horse ride with an instructor's supervision.

ⓐ Turaidas 10, Sigulda. **ⓣ** 926 84 57. **ⓛ** 10.00–20.00.

Hot air balloon rides

Gently drift over the scenic Gauja Valley and the towns of Cesis and Sigulda.

ⓐ Mukusalas iela 41, Riga. **ⓣ** 761 16 14. **ⓦ** www.altius.lv

Biplane sightseeing

Take to the air in an AN-2, the world's largest biplane, and soar over the scenic Gauja Valley. Or be really daring and take a parachute jump from 700 m (2300 ft).

ⓐ Cesis Airfield. **ⓣ** 642 91 68.

Paintball

Stalk your friends and loved ones on two courses, one in the woods with natural obstacles, the other in an open field with car tires as obstructions.

ⓐ Priekuli Parish. **ⓣ** 922 45 89.

RETAIL THERAPY

Griezi Crafts Salon Filled with local souvenirs and works of local artists. **ⓐ** Rigas iela 17a, Cesis.

TAKING A BREAK

Buca Mario Pizzeria Tiny and sparsely decorated, this one-room pizzeria serves a variety of thin-crust pizzas and a few pasta dishes. A biscuit accompanies tea or coffee to finish off your meal. **ⓐ** Pils 4b, Sigulda. **ⓣ** 797 33 22. **ⓛ** Daily 11.00–23.00.

Tris Draugi A budget traveller's buffet dream. Good and cheap food such as shashliks, beef stroganoff and pork chops served up in modest surroundings. **ⓐ** Pils 9, Sigulda. **ⓣ** 797 37 21. **ⓛ** Daily 08.00–22.00.

ⓞ *Anyone can try out the exhilarating sport of bobsleigh*

Kaku Maja (Cat House) Cosy little bistro and bar serving a good selection of Latvian staples and some salad selections for those seeking healthier fare. The beer selection is modest, the interior rustic, and the aromas from the adjoining bakery are tempting. ⓐ Pils 8, Sigulda. ⓛ Daily 08.00–23.00.

Aroma A cosy coffee shop right in the centre of Cesis, next to the square. ⓐ Lencu iela 4, Cesis. ⓣ 412 75 75.

AFTER DARK

Restaurants
Admiraju Klubs £ Dark, smoky and filled with gamblers. The major attraction is the slots, but you'll also find four pool tables, two snooker tables and air hockey and football. Everything for a guy's night out. ⓐ Pils 12, Sigulda. ⓛ Mon–Thu 10.00–22.00, Fri- Sat 10.00–04.00.

Melnais Kakis £ A smaller cousin to the one in Riga, this establishment caters to all your tastes – a wide menu selection, pool table and slot machines in the back. A good way to while away an evening in the countryside. ⓐ Pils 8, Sigulda. ⓣ 915 01 04. ⓛ Daily 11.00–04.00.

Aparjods £–££ Modelled on a traditional farmstead and decorated with antique clocks and bric-a-brac, this is the best place to have dinner in Sigulda. Ask for a table near the wood-burning fireplace and be prepared to try a menu that carries everything from stuffed pheasant to lobster. ⓐ Ventas 1a, Sigulda. ⓣ 770 52 42. ⓛ Daily 12.00–01.00.

ACCOMMODATION

Aparjods £ An enthusiastic mix of rural and rustic Latvian influences seamlessly combined with modern conveniences such as satellite TV and whirlpool. Only 14 rooms on site.
ⓐ Ventas 1b, Sigulda. ⓣ 797 22 30. ⓕ 797 22 30. ⓦ www.aparjods.lv

Ezeri £ Brightly and tastefully decorated, this small hotel exudes the charm you would expect from an out-of-city location. Spend a weekend in the country fishing, cycling, or even horse riding.
ⓐ Siguldas pagasts, Sigulda. ⓣ 797 30 09. ⓕ 797 38 80.

Livkalns £ A winding gravel road leads you away from the hustle and bustle to the quiet retreat of this hotel. Only eight rooms and a restaurant, but a real find. ⓐ Peteralas 3, Sigulda.

Santa £–££ A modern and cosy hotel just outside the city that offers comfortable rooms with a great view of the lake, a bar, restaurant, sauna and a small swimming pool.
ⓐ Kainjani, Sigulda.
ⓣ 770 52 71. ⓕ 770 52 78.

Sigulda ££ The most central hotel in Sigulda has recently been renovated and is now even bigger and better than before. The rooms are modern and spacious. ⓐ Pils 6, Sigulda. ⓣ 797 22 63. ⓕ 797 14 43.

🔺 *The farmstead restaurant of Aparjods*

Western Latvia

Do you fancy a day trip to long sandy beaches or deep squelchy forest bogs? Maybe some time spent viewing the lavish excesses of some 18th-century dukes? Most of Western Latvia's tourist attractions are within an easy day trip of Riga.

Begin with a trip to the Zemgale region, an area that extends south of Riga to the Lithuanian border. Although the landscape is largely flat and somewhat uninteresting, it is decorated with two sumptuous palaces – the neo-classical Mezotne and the baroque-rococo Rundale Palace. Both palaces are within easy reach of Bauska and all three places can be visited in a single day.

Kurzeme is home to some of Latvia's most spectacular natural scenery. The coast road west from Riga is a ribbon that runs along an unspoiled coast to where the Baltic Sea meets the Gulf of Riga. This area is filled with intriguing towns waiting to be explored and spectacular and varied landscapes.

Kuldiga, filled with medieval atmosphere and charm, has existed since at least the 9th century, but it was not until the German invaders of the 13th century arrived that a castle and other significant buildings were established. Over the centuries the town grew, and todays the town' pride is the preserved architecture and bridge constructions. The Old Town Hall and Town Square, built in the 17th century, is the centrepiece of the town. The houses in the town were created with decorated front doors and skylight windows above.

Liepaja is possibly the furthest you will travel in Latvia while using Riga as your base. This is a city that embraces its maritime traditions. The lighthouses of Liepaja were most likely the first ones to welcome European sailors, as people have lived in this area for

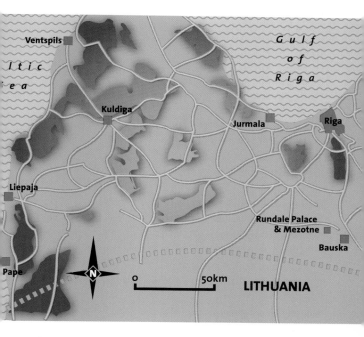

Ventspils

Gulf
of
Riga

ltic
ea

Kuldiga

Jurmala

Riga

Liepaja

Rundale Palace
& Mezotne

Bauska

Pape

0   50km

LITHUANIA

N

more than 750 years. At one time the city was the capital of Latvia, and it has a unique heritage of being governed by Swedish kings, German barons, Russian tsars and Finnish *jeegers*.

A visit to the seashore, or *jurmala,* of the Liepaja region is a real surprise. Thanks to the presence of the Soviet Army for almost 50 years, this area has remained largely untouched. Take some time to wander the empty beaches backed by juniper and pine trees. And, if the wind is right, you may even find some amber that has been washed on to the shore.

SIGHTS & ATTRACTIONS

Rundale Palace

Make sure you find time on your schedule to visit this beautiful Baroque palace. It was originally designed by Italian architect, Francesco Bartolomeo, the designer of St Petersburg's Winter Palace. The building took more than 28 years to build and decorate. This palace was once part of the fortune of the Duke of Courland. There is a restaurant in the museum.

a Pilsrundale, Bauska. **t** 396 21 97. **w** www.rpm.apollo.lv **l** Daily 10.00–16.00.

Museum of Fishery & Navigation

This intriguing museum is located in the former mansion of Captain Gvido Grinvalds, in the Liepaja Maritime Park. You'll find more than 7000 items relating to saltwater and inland fishery and navigation, and a sizeable fleet of model ships.

a Hikes iela 9, Liepaja. **t** 342 69 96. **l** Daily 11.00–18.00.

Wild Horses of Lake Pape

Polski Konik wild horses have been living in the meadows of Lake Pape since 1999 and now number more than 50. Excursions with a guide are arranged with the World Wide Fund for Nature. The tour lasts about an hour and you should be prepared to walk about 2km (1½ miles). **a** Lake Pape, Pape. **t** 948 97 75.

◗ *This region's lighthouses symbolise Latvia's maritime heritage*

CULTURE

Like all good cities, Liepaja contradicts itself culturally. Home to the oldest professional theatre in Latvia and to the only symphony orchestra in the country, it also numbers more rock musicians per head of population than any other place in the country. Whatever your cultural tastes, you're sure to find it covered in Liepaja.

Liepaja Theatre The oldest professional theatre in all Latvia, founded in 1917, performs mostly musicals for both adults and children. ⓐ Teatra iela 4, Liepaja. ❶ 342 01 45. Ⓦ www.teatris.liepajanet.lv

Symphony Orchestra Liepaja is the only city in Latvia that has its own symphony orchestra, which is one of the oldest in the Baltic States. It frequently debuts new music by Latvian composers. ⓐ 50 Gradu iela, Liepaja. ❶ 342 55 38. Ⓦ www.lso.apollo.lv

The Gallery Rozu laukums Art exhibitions of local artists and crafts people are on display. The Gallery shop also has a good selection of souvenirs. ⓐ 5–6 Rozu laukums, Liepaja. ❶ 342 25 67. ❻ Mon–Fri 10.00–19.00, Sat 10.00–17.00, Sun 11.00–14.00.

Artists' workshops A list of artists' workshops that can be visited is available from the Liepaja tourist board. Most of these require booking in advance. Ⓦ www.liepaja.lv

RETAIL THERAPY

Peter's Market This covered market is an excellent location at which to pick up the ingredients of an impromptu picnic. Countrywomen from the region bring milk, eggs, potatoes and gooseberries into town for this regular market. Buy a *sklandarausis* (a cake of rye flour, potatoes and carrots) and indulge in the authentic taste of the latvian countryside. ⓐ Liepaja.

Lauma Is the largest textile company in Eastern Europe. Its speciality? Lingerie. Slinky, silky lingerie for 'evening' wear and beautifully crafted, seamless sports wear. And, yes, there are tablecloths, towels, sheets and pillowcases, too. ⓐ 12 L iela, Liepaja. 🕐 Mon–Fri 10.00–18.00, Sat: 10.00–15.00.

Craftsmen's House Various craftsmen and folk artists work is gathered in this location. Items of amber, weavings, knitted items and other handicrafts are offered for sale. ⓐ 33 Barinu iela, Liepaja. 🕐 Mon–Fri, 11.00–18.00

TAKING A BREAK

Pastnieka Maja (Postman's House) A glass wall separates you from the passing pedestrians and trams while you sip a blackberry or linden tea. The menu? Open the yellow envelope to make your selection, from a small snack to a substantial local specialty. ⓐ 55 Brivzemnieka iela, Liepaja. ☎ 340 75 21. 🕐 Daily 12.00–24.00.

Liepajas Maiznieks (Liepaja's Bakery) The aromas wafting from the open windows of the city's oldest bakery will draw you from hundreds of metres away. Throw your diet to the wind and try some of the 'Sono' confectionary of little treats or buy some of the hearty wholegrain bread or rolls for a picnic. ⓐ 62 Klaipedas iela, Liepaja.

● *Dine to a postal theme at Pastnieka Maja*

Livu Alus Sip a Latvian beer while watching it being made in the largest brewery in Latvia. ❷ 9-11 Ganibu iela, Liepaja. ❶ 342 23 53. ◐ Daily 12.00–24.00.

Livu Akvaparks Latvia's largest indoor aquapark, open all year round, includes a wave pool, water slides and a children's pool. When you're tired of splashing about in the water there's a bar and restaurant to restore your energy. ❷ Vienibas gatve 36, Liepaja. ❶ 775 56 40. ◐ Daily 12.00–23.00.

AFTER DARK

Big 7 A multi-dimensional recreation hall that holds up to 600 people, just in case you want to bring a few friends. Topless dancing, 'go-go dancing', martinis, billiards, gambling and a light show. Who

could ask for anything more? ⓐ 14–16 Baznicas iela, Liepaja.
ⓣ 342 73 18.

1st Rock Café £ Definitely a Hard Rock Café-wannabe. Nevertheless it's a good place to play billiards, listen to music and gaze at rock memorabilia. ⓐ 18–20 Stendera iela, Liepaja. ⓣ 348 15 55.
ⓦ www.pablo.lv ⓛ 07.00–19.00 (24 hrs in summer).

Devitais Vilnis (The Ninth Wave) £ Can't decide what kind of food you'd like to eat? This café specialises in foods from many ports of call. You'll find almost everything from Chinese to Spanish on the menu. ⓐ 21 Celtnieku iela, Liepaja. ⓣ 340 14 45.

Barons Bumbieris ££ A traditional, medieval themed, restaurant that scores high with its generous renditions of pork ribs and sauerkraut. L iela 13, Kurzeme Shopping Centre, Liepaja.
ⓣ 342 54 11. ⓛ Daily 09.00–24.00.

ACCOMMODATION

Chill Inn £ A funky beach house only 500 metres from the sea, and a mere 10km from Liepaja. Board walks, small tables, comfortable rooms and a friendly atmosphere. ⓐ Bernati, Nica Parish.
ⓣ 642 58 00. ⓦ www.chillinn.lv

K@2 Youth Hostel £ A short walk to the beach, clean dorm rooms, access to the internet and breakfast included. Just about all you could want in a hostel. Make sure to call ahead to ensure that someone will be there to let you in. ⓐ Katedraies iela 2, Liepaja.
ⓣ 974 79 62.

Liva £–££ Don't judge a book by its cover, or in this case, a hotel by its facade. The exterior may be a bit dingy but the rooms have been recently renovated and the location couldn't be more central. Private bathrooms, cable TV, telephone and writing desks in each room. There is also a restaurant and two bars on site. **ⓐ** L iela 11, Liepaja. **ⓣ** 342 01 02. **ⓕ** 348 02 59.

The Fontaine Hotel £–££ Quirky and sometimes garish, the Fontaine is a fun place to stay. The rooms are an eclectic mix of hardwood floors with oriental carpets adorned with army footlockers for tables. The decor can only be described as exuberant. The rooms also include cable TV, DVD players, and private bathrooms. If you want a room with a balcony be sure to book far in advance. **ⓐ** Juras iela 24, Liepaja. **ⓣ** 342 09 56. **ⓕ** 342 09 56.

Roze Guest House £–££ A turn-of-the-century art nouveau guest house only 100m from the sea. The decor whisks you away to a gentler time but contemporary amenities assure your stay will be comfortable. **ⓐ** 37 Rozu iela , Liepaja. **ⓣ** 342 11 55. **ⓦ** www.parkhotel-rose.lv

Amrita ££–£££ A four-star hotel opened in 1997 is a favourite of foreign and local businessmen. Single and double rooms offer satellite TV, telephone, showers and hairdryer. There's also a two-storey suite with a whirlpool, provided the president isn't in town. **ⓐ** Rigas iela 7/9, Liepaja. **ⓣ** 340 34 34. **ⓕ** 348 04 44.

▶ *Make Riga's helpful tourist information office your first stop on arrival*

PRACTICAL
information

Directory

GETTING THERE
By air
The easiest way to get to Riga is to fly. Riga International Airport is fully modern and highly rated among European airports. It is served by direct flights from 34 cities in Europe, Asia and America. Riga is served by daily flights from most major cities in Europe. Direct flights depart from Amsterdam, Barcelona, Berlin, Brussels, Cologne, Copenhagen, Dublin, Istanbul, Frankfurt, Geneva, Hamburg, Helsinki, Kiev, London, Manchester, Milan, Minsk, Moscow, Munich, New York, Oslo, Prague, Stockholm, Stuttgart, Tallinn, Tampere, Tashkent, Tel Aviv, Vienna, Vilnius and Warsaw. Low-cost air services from the UK to Riga are offered by:

Air Baltic Ⓦ www.airbaltic.lv
Easyjet Ⓦ www.easyjet.com
Estonian Air Ⓦ www.estonianair.ee
Ryanair Ⓦ www.ryanair.com

By train
There is a direct service from Vilnius in Lithuania and from several Russian cities. Services are available from the rest of Europe via Vilnius. The train service in Latvia is among the worst in Europe, as it has not been properly maintained or upgraded in recent years. Eurail passes are not valid in Latvia. The monthly *Thomas Cook European Rail Timetable* has up-to-date schedules for European international and Latvian train services.

Riga Central Railway Station is located just outside the south-east end of the Old Town at Stacijas laukums. It has been recently renovated, and has currency exchange, ATM, shops, a post office, ticket booths, restaurants and a news-stand. Unless you have heavy luggage it is easier to leave on foot, as many of the major hotels are within a 10-minute walk, but taxis can be flagged just outside the station. A taxi to anywhere in the Old Town or City Centre should not cost more than 3 to 5 Lats.

Thomas Cook European Rail Timetable (UK) 01733 416477; (USA) 1 800 322 3834. www.thomascookpublishing.com

Driving

Driving from the UK can take a long time, the total distance from Calais being about 2160 km (1342 miles). The roads are good and fast through Western Europe, but once you reach Poland the pace will slow, as there are few multilane fast highways in Poland and the Baltic states.

By bus

If you want someone else to do the driving, bus is preferable to train. The main long-distance bus terminal is located at the south-east end of the Old Town, just one block away from the railway station. There is a regular service from Tallinn and Vilnius, with connections to most other major European cities. The bus terminal has currency exchange, ATMs, a news-stand, a drug store, and a restaurant. Taxis can be flagged just outside the terminal and should not cost more than 3 to 5 Lats to anywhere in the Old Town or city centre (which is only a short walk away if you don't have heavy luggage).

By ferry

The Ferry Terminal is located about 1 km north-west of the Old Town. There are ferry connections from Stockholm by Riga Sea Line (temporarily suspended at time of writing) and from Kiel and Lübeck connecting with the UK (three times per week to and from Harwich). The Ferry Terminal has currency exchange, an ATM and a restaurant. Trams 5, 7 and 9 leave from in front of the terminal, and will take you to the Old Town and to the City Centre. The cost is only 0.20L, and tickets can be purchased directly from the driver. Taxis are available just outside the terminal entrance. A ride to the Old Town or city centre should take about 10 minutes, and cost about 5 Lats.

Riga Sea Line Ⓦ www.rigasealine.lv
DFDS Tor Line Ⓦ www.dfds.com

🔽 *Many tourists arrive at Riga's passenger terminal*

ENTRY FORMALITIES

Documentation

A valid passport is required to enter the country. Since Latvia joined the EU in 2004, entry into the country has become very easy for most people. Entry from another EU country is normally very quick, although entry from Russia can take some time. Citizens of Canada, Australia, New Zealand and the USA, and of EU-member states, do not require a visa unless they plan to stay longer than 90 days. Citizens of most other countries, including South Africa, will require a visa, available on entry at Riga airport but not at land borders.

Customs

The import of guns, narcotics, pornography and other normally banned material is forbidden. There are no restrictions on the amount of hard currency you can bring in or take out. Exporting items from Latvia is easy unless the object dates from before 1945, in which case the item is taxed and also requires an export permit issued by the Ministry of Culture (ⓐ Pils 22, Riga).

MONEY

The national currency is the Latvian Lat. At the time of writing L1 equals about £1. The Lat is broken down into 100 santimi. There are coins of 1, 2, 5, 10, 20, and 50 santimi, and of 1 and 2 Lats. There are banknotes of 5, 10, 20, 50, 100 and 500 Lats.

Traveller's cheques and Eurocheques can be exchanged in banks. Note that foreign banknotes that are torn, marked with ink, or very old are only accepted at considerable discount, or not at all.

Most larger hotels, stores and restaurants accept Visa, MasterCard, Eurocard, Diner's Club and American Express. Many shops and restaurants, especially those frequented by tourists, will accept euros and some charge in euros, which is why some prices are quoted thus in this book. However, it is always advisable to carry some Lats with you.

Banks and ATMs are plentiful and easy to find in Riga. All banks offer currency exchange. Exchange offices are also found in larger hotels, the airport, railway station, passenger port, and major shopping centres.

HEALTH, SAFETY & CRIME

Latvia is relatively low-risk in terms of health problems. No immunisations are required before visiting, although if you plan to hike in wooded or boggy areas you should be vaccinated against tick-borne encephalitis. This presents itself as a rash, possibly with flu-like symptons, and left untreated it can have long-term effects: if you have any reason to think that you have contracted it from a tick, seek immediate treatment. To protect yourself, cover up legs and arms when walking in long grass and if a tick does attach itself to you remove it at once.

The tap water is safe to drink, although it is frequently less than palatable. The food in almost all restaurants is properly prepared and safe to eat.

Minor ailments can usually be treated at pharmacies (*aptieka*), which carry a wide range of international drugs from pain killers to antibiotics. Major complaints are best treated at a hospital (*slimnica*). Emergency treatment is free but if you are admitted to hospital you will be charged a fee for bed space and drugs.

The standard of medical care is high, and not a cause for concern. Most doctors speak English, but other health care workers may not. There are private clinics with English-speaking doctors in Riga – see Emergencies on page 156 for details. EU reciprocal health care privileges apply in Latvia: UK residents should obtain a European Health Insurance Card (EHIC) before travelling. However, it is still wise (and for visitors from outside the EU, absolutely essential) to take out comprehensive travel insurance with good health cover.

Latvia has a relatively low crime rate. However, tourist attractions, such as Old Town, are prime hunting grounds for sneak thieves, muggers and pickpockets. Try to keep mobile phones and

● *If you need a policeman, look for a man in blue*

camera equipment out of sight as much as possible, and leave expensive jewellery at home. If you have a car, be sure to park it in a guarded and well lit lot, as car theft is common. You should not walk the streets alone after dark. There have been reports of racist attacks on Latvian residents who come from from Africa and Asia.

If you are the victim of crime, be patient with the police. Many officers, especially the older ones, are not fluent in English. The police are generally courteous and businesslike, but can be slow in filling out crime report forms. They are generally unsympathetic to foreign drivers who break traffic regulations and will insist on applying on-the-spot fines. Make a copy of your passport and other important travel documents such as air tickets. If these items are

One of Riga's old town clocks will help you keep an eye on opening hours

lost, replacement will be much easier with these copies at hand.

Visitors are required to carry identification at all times, although it is unlikely that you will be required to produce it except when entering and leaving the country.

OPENING HOURS

You'll find the majority of business establishments are open from 08.00 to 17.00, with a leisurely hour taken off at lunch. Lunch is, in fact, the main meal of the day in Latvia, so expect restaurants and eateries to be quite busy between 13.00 and 15.00. Banks are normally open from 09.00 to 18.00 on weekdays, while some are also open on Saturday from 10.00 to 15.00. Shops generally stay open until 18.00, some later on Thursday and Friday evenings, keeping limited hours on Saturday and closing completely on Sunday. The exception are grocery stores, which open for a few hours on Sunday.

TOILETS

Brush up on the correct symbols to avoid embarrassment. Men's facilities are designated by a V, a K, or a triangle pointing downward. Women should look for an S, a D, or a triangle pointing upward.

A surprisingly clean and tidy exception to the generally poor public toilet situation are the facilities in the newly renovated central train station. Most hotels or restaurants are pretty accommodating about allowing you to use their loos without being a customer.

CHILDREN

Riga may not be the best city to bring young children to visit. Older ones may enjoy parts of the city that look as though they have stepped from their history and story books. Finding smoke-free and family- friendly eateries may be a bit of a challenge and the cobble-stoned streets of the Old Town will definitely throw some navigational challenges in the way of your pushchair.

Good places for kids Include:

- **Latvian State Puppet Theatre** Puppetry remains a strong art in many parts of Europe and the plays presented here are top notch. Very young children, from ages 2-6, will benefit the most from this type of performance. A nice feature is that the chair height will adjust so that even the smallest child will still have a good view of the stage. ⓐ Kr. Barona iela 16/18. ⓣ 728 53 55. ⓦ www.puppet.lv

- **Riga Circus** The Riga Circus is the only permanent circus in the Baltics. It features some unusual acts including performing pigs and domestic cats that don't always care to perform. But children of all ages always enjoy a circus. ⓐ Merkela 4. ⓣ 721 32 79. ⓦ www.cirks.lv

- **Riga Zoo** Set in a pine-tree forest the Riga Zoo is a remarkably varied zoo with all the standard zoo fare such as polar bears and some intriguing inclusions like Tibetan wild donkeys and an insect centre. The zoo and the surrounding Forest Park is a favourite strolling area for residents. ⓐ Meza Prospekts 1. ⓣ 751 86 69. ⓛ 10.00–18.00. ⓦ www.rigazoo.lv

- **Open-air Ethnographic Museum** 100 hectares of Latvian life as it was once upon a time. Farmsteads, fishing villages, windmills and churches have been relocated to this open -air museum to be preserved for posterity. Craftsmen offer daily demonstrations.

- **Lido Relaxation Centre** This giant centre houses a huge skating rink, lots of children's attractions. ❸ Krasta 76. ❶ 750 44 20. ❹ Daily 10.00–23.00.

- **Liva Akvaparks Jurmala** Kiddie's pool, wave pools, six water slides and a tubing river will keep children of all ages happy all day long. The largest water park in Latvia, complete with a restaurant and bar. ❷ Vienibas gatve 36, Lielupe, Jurmala. ❶ 775 56 40. ❹ Daily 12.00–23.00.

◗ Children will be enchanted by the many traditional toys and puppets

- **Vairak Saules** A kids' menu and all the Lego a child's heart could desire in a smoke-free environment. ⓐ Dzirnavu 60. ⓣ 728 28 78.

- **Spotikacs** Colouring books, and a tree with a TV inside showing cartoons. ⓐ Antonijas 12, Riga. ⓣ 750 59 55.

COMMUNICATIONS

Phones

The telephone system in Latvia is reliable and easy to use. All numbers within the country are seven-digit and there are no area codes. Riga has a good supply of public telephone boxes, but they use magnetic cards and not coins. The public phones offer international direct dialling, and many have English language instructions posted inside. . If you will be using a pay phone, you can purchase a Lattelekom card (ⓦ www.lattelekom.lv). These are available in values of €2, 3, and 5 These are available for both national and international calls, and can be purchased at news-stands, post offices and some stores.

If you have a GSM mobile phone, it is possible to avoid heavy roaming charges by purchasing a prepaid SIM card from one of the local services, such as Amiga or Zelta Zivtina. Starter packs and refills are available at newspaper kiosks and grocery stores.

Calling into and out of Latvia is easy. To call in, simply dial your country's international access code, then 371 (Latvia's country code) and then the seven-digit number. To call out, dial 00, then the country code and then the local number (omitting the first 0 in the case of UK area codes).

Post

The Latvian postal system is quite reliable. The main Riga Post Office is conveniently located at ⓐ Stacijas laukums, just south-east of the

Old Town, and near both the railway station and bus terminal. There are other post offices in the city centre, including ⓐ Brivibas iela 19 and ⓐ Elizabetes iela 41/43.

Besides handling mail and stamps, the post office can be used to send and receive faxes, and to make international telephone calls. Telegrams can be sent 24 hours a day by telephoning 900 2178.

Sending a letter to Europe costs 0.20 Lats, and to North American and Australasia costs 0.25 Lats.

Information on postal services ☏ 800 8001 ⓦ www.riga.post.lv

Internet

Riga and other large cities in Latvia are well served by internet cafés, although in smaller towns they may be difficult to find. Internet access is also available in public libraries, but be prepared to queue for a terminal. Here are some of the most central internet points in Riga:

Delat 14 computers. Snacks, beverages and alcohol are available. If you need a scanner you'll find it here, at an extra cost. Cost: 0.60 Lats an hour. ⓐ Baznicas 4a, Riga. ☏ 722 05 10. ⏰ 24 hours.

Dualnet Café 15 computers on site. 0.80–1 Lats per hour, varying with the time of day. ⓐ Peldu 17, Riga. ☏ 781 44 40. ⏰ 24 hours.

Planeta Have to stop mid-sightseeing to check your email? This Old Town location has four rooms of computers. Cost: 0.45 Lats per hour. ⓐ Pils 14, Riga. ☏ 722 66 73. ⏰ 24 hours.

Skonto Datu Sistema (Bliteks) Eight computers, beer, wine, and alcohol. Cost: 0.50 Lats for 15 min. ⓐ Elizabetes iela 75, Riga. ☏ 728 28 76. ⏰ Daily 09.30–22.00, 10.00–20.00 Sat–Sun.

MEDIA
Television
Many hotels are equipped with a wide range of cable channels offering programs in English, German and Russian. Most locals tune in to state-owned channels LTV1 and LYV7 for serious news and culture, and to privately-owned LNT and TV3 for game shows and dramas. English language films are shown on LTV7 with Latvian subtitles.

Radio stations
In Riga, you get a wide range of music, from progressive rock to golden oldies to classical:
BBC (100.5 FM) Virtual heaven for World Service fanatics. BBC in English 24 hours a day.

Classical Music (103.7 FM)

European Hit Radio (104.3 FM) Mostly techno and European hits.

Latvian National Radio 1 (90.7 FM) English-language Latvian news, 20.00–20.30; in Swedish from 21.30–22.00.

SWH (105.2 FM) A Riga favourite. SWH in Russian is at 89.2; music and news.

Super FM (104.3 FM) The most popular station in Riga. Plays mostly techno.

Magazines and newspapers
The weekly English-language magazine *Riga This Week* is available

at tourist information offices, hotels, restaurants and the airport, and is a good source of information on entertainment and events and of restaurant reviews. The main newspaper for expatriates is the *Baltic Times*, available at news-stands.

Latvia boasts a wide array of magazines and newspapers for a country of only 1.5 million inhabitants. If your Latvian language skills aren't quite up to speed, *Studjia* is an excellent fine arts magazine with English summaries.

ELECTRICITY

The electrical system in Latvia is very reliable. It is 220 volts AC, 50 hertz. The plug is two pin, European style. Travellers from the UK will need to take adapters with them for their 3-pin appliances; North American visitors will need a transformer. It is easier to purchase these items before setting off than to find a shop selling them in Riga.

TRAVELLERS WITH DISABILITIES

The Baltic States have a long way to go to become truly wheelchair-accessible, or even -friendly. Even in the larger cities access to public transport and tourist attractions is sadly lacking.

Tourist offices can be especially helpful in determining if there is suitable accommodation if you make your request in advance. It's a good idea to double-check any information you receive, as some establishments will advertise services that are still to be implemented. Normally, the larger and more modern the hotel the better the provision for disabled guests is likely to be.

If you travel with a wheelchair have it serviced before your departure and carry any essentials you may need to affect repairs. It is also a good idea to travel with any spares of special clothing or

equipment that might be difficult to replace. Associations dealing with your particular disability can be excellent sources of information on conditions and circumstances in other countries. The following contacts may be helpful.

United Kingdom & Republic of Ireland
Tripscope ⓐ Alexandra House, Albany Road. Brentford, Middlesex, TW8 0NE. ❶ 0845 758 5641. Ⓦ www.tripscope.org.uk

Irish Wheelchair Association ⓐ Blackheath Drive, Clontarf. Dublin 3. ❶ 01 818 6400. Ⓦ www.iwa.ie

USA & Canada
Society for the Advancement of Travelers with Handicaps (SATH)
ⓐ 347 5th Avenue. New York, NY 10016. ❶ 212/447-7284. Ⓦ www.sath.org

Access-able Ⓦ www.access-able.com

Australia & New Zealand
Australian Council for Rehabilitation of the Disabled (ACROD)
ⓐ PO Box 60. Curtin, ACT 2605, Australia. ❶ 02 6282 4333. Ⓦ www.acrod.org.au

Disabled Persons Assembly ⓐ 173–175 Victoria Street. Wellington, NZ. ❶ 04 801 9100. Ⓦ www.dpa.org.nz

TOURIST INFORMATION
Tourist offices
City of Riga Information Centre Very helpful tourist information

centre that offers a wide range of information in a variety of languages. Can assist with hotel bookings and other useful services. ⓐ Ratslaukums 6, Riga. ☎ 704 43 77. 🖶 704 43 78. 📧 tourinfo@rcc.lv 🌐 www.rigatourism.com 🕐 10.00–19.00

There are also branches at the central bus station and central rail station:

Bus station: ⓐ Pragas iela 1 ☎ 722 05 55. 🕐 09.00–19.00.

Rail station: ⓐ Stacijas iela 2. ☎ 723 38 15. 🕐 10.00–18.30.

Latvian Tourist Information Centre This bureau is very useful if you intend to explore outside the city on one of the out of town trips. It can provide maps and useful advice as well as arrange hotel reservations. ⓐ Smilsu iela 4. ☎ 722 46 64. 🖶 722 46 65. 📧 info@latviatourism.lv 🌐 http://latviatourism.lv 🕐 09.00–18.00.

Useful websites

Apart from the websites of the two tourist offices listed above, the following official and unofficial websites are all good sources of information for planning your trip:

🌐 **www.virtualriga.lv** Topical city and news guide

🌐 **www.inspirationriga.lv** Official site of Riga Tourism

🌐 **www.rigathisweek.com** Up-to-date listings of arts, culture, restaurants and accommodations.

🌐 **www.lv** General directory of Latvian resources on the web

🌐 **www.art.lv** Listings of galleries, with links to artists

🌐 **www.cultre.lv** Lots of links to Riga's cultural life

🌐 **www.folklora.lv** The scoop on the Latvian folk scene

🌐 **www.virtual.lv** City plans and maps on line

🌐 **www.hostellinglatvia.com** Listings of hostels.

LANGUAGE

Useful phrases

Although English is spoken by the personnel of many tourist services , these Latvian words and phrases may come in handy. See also the phrases for specific situations in other parts of the book.

English	Latvian	*Approx. pronunciation*
BASICS		
Yes	Jā	*Ja*
No	Nē	*Ne*
Please	Lūdzu	*Ludzu*
Thank you	Paldies	*Paldies*
Hello	Sveiki	*Sveiki*
Goodbye	Uz redzēšanos	*Uz redzeshanos*
Excuse me	Atvainojiet	*Atvaynoyiet*
Sorry	Piedodiet	*Piedodiet*
That's O.K.	Tas ir labi	*Tas ir labi*
To	Līdz	*Lidz*
From	No	*No*
I don't speak Latvian	Es nerunāju latviski	*Es nerunayu latviski*
Do you speak English?	Vai Jūs runājat angliski?	*Vai Jus runayat angliski?*
Good morning	Labrīt	*Labrit*
Good afternoon	Labdien	*Labdien*
Good evening	Labvakar	*Labvakar*
Good night	Ar labunakti	*Ar labunakti*
My name is ...	Mans vārds ir ...	*Mans vahrds ir ...*
DAYS & TIMES		
Monday	Pirmdiena	*Pirmdiena*
Tuesday	Otrdiena	*Otrdiena*
Wednesday	Trešdiena	*Treshdiena*
Thursday	Ceturtdiena	*Tseturdiena*
Friday	Piektdiena	*Piekdiena*
Saturday	Sestdiena	*Sesdiena*
Sunday	Svētdiena	*Svediena*
Morning	Rīts	*Rits*
Afternoon	Pēcpusdiena	*Petspusdiena*
Evening	Vakars	*Vakars*
Night	Nakts	*Nakts*
Yesterday	Vakar	*Vakar*

English	Latvian	*Approx. pronunciation*
Today	Šodien	*Shuodien*
Tomorrow	Rīt	*Rit*
What time is it?	Cik ir pulkstenis?	*Tsik ir pulkstenis?*
It is ...	Pulkstenis ir...	*Pulkstenis ir...*
9.00	Deviņi	*Devini*
Midday	Dienasvidus	*Dienasvidus*
Midnight	Pusnakts	*Pusnakts*

NUMBERS

One	Viens	*Viens*
Two	Divi	*Divi*
Three	Trīs	*Tris*
Four	Četri	*Tshetri*
Five	Pieci	*Pietsi*
Six	Seši	*Seshi*
Seven	Septiņi	*Septini*
Eight	Astoņi	*Astoni*
Nine	Deviņi	*Devini*
Ten	Desmit	*Desmit*
Twenty	Divdesmit	*Divdesmit*
Fifty	Piecdesmit	*Pietsdesmit*
One hundred	Simts	*Simts*

MONEY

I would like to change these traveller's cheques/this currency	Es vēlos izmainīt šos ceļojumu čekus/šo valūtu	*Es velos izmainit shos tselyoyumu chekus/scho valutu*
Where is the nearest ATM?	Kur ir tuvākais bankas automāts?	*Kur ir tuvahkais bankas automahts?*
Do you accept credit cards?	Vai jūs pieņemat kredītkartes?	*Vai yus pienemat kreditkartes?*

SIGNS & NOTICES

Airport	Lidosta	*Lidosta*
Ladies/Gentlemen	Dāmām/Kungiem	*Damam/Kungiem*
Platform	Dzelzceļa stacijas perons	*Dzelztselya statsiyas perons*
Railway station	Dzelzceļa stacija	*Dzelztselya statsiya*
Smoking/ Non-smoking	Smēķēt atļauts/ Smēķēt aizliegts	*Smeket atlyauts/ Smeket aizliegts*
Police station	Policijas iecirknis	*Politsiyas ietsirknis*

155

Emergencies

EMERGENCY NUMBERS
In an emergency call:
Fire 01
Police 02
Ambulance 03
Pan-European Assistance 112 This number will connect you with someone to assist you in English.

MEDICAL EMERGENCIES
There are increasingly professional options for general medical treatment. Some Western-trained doctors have set up private practices in Riga, for instance.

Hospitals
Hospital No 1 ⓐ Bruninieku iela 5. ⓣ 727 04 91 ⓦ www.1slimnica.lv
University children`s hospital ⓐ Vienibas iela 45. ⓣ 706 44 99.
ⓦ www.bkus.lv
Hospital Gailezers ⓐ Hipokrata iela 2. ⓣ 704 24 24 ⓦ www.gailes.lv
Paul Stradinsh Clinical Hospital ⓐ Pilsonu iela 13, ⓣ 706 96 01.
ⓦ www.stradini.lv

Doctor
ARS Clinic Has a 24-hour service in English, ⓐ Skolas iela 5.
ⓣ 720 10 08.

Dentists
Republican Dental Outpatient Hospital ⓐ Dzirciema 20. ⓣ 781 5320.
ⓦ www.st-inst.lv

Elladent ❷ Vilandes 18. ☎ 733 31 45.
Sandent ❷ Blaumana 3. ☎ 728 03 71

EMBASSIES & CONSULATES
Australia ❷ Raina bulv. 3, Riga. ☎ 722 23 88.
Canada ❷ Doma laukums 4, Riga. ☎ 722 63 15,
New Zealand Contact UK embassy.
Republic of Ireland ❸ Brivibas iela 54. ☎ 702 25 222.
South Africa Contact UK embassy.
UK ❷ Alunana iela 5, Riga. ☎ 777 47 00.
USA ❷ Raina bulv. 7, Riga. ☎ 703 62 00.

EMERGENCY PHRASES

Help! Palīgā! *Paliga!*

Fire! Deg! *Degs!*

Stop! Stāt! *Stat!*

Call an ambulance/a doctor/ the police/the fire service!
Izsauciet ātro palīdzību/ārstu/ policiju/ugunsdzēsēju komandu!
Izsautsiet atro palidzibu/arstu/ politsiyu/ugunsdzeseyu komandu!

INDEX

The publishers would like to thank the following individuals and organisations for supplying their copyright photographs for this book.
A1 Pix: pages 1, 5, 15, 17, 20, 21, 23, 40/41, 47, 59, 66, 69, 81, 83, 90/91, 99, 101, 104/105, 113, 117, 121, 127, 131, 137, 144, 147.
Ann Carroll Burgess & Tom Burgess: pages 7, 19, 24, 72, 87, 89, 140.
Stillman Rogers Photography: pages 29, 37, 44, 63, 134.
Latvia Tourism: pages 13, 31, 125, 143.

Proofreader: Janet McCann
Copy-editor: Deborah Parker

Send your thoughts to
books@thomascook.com

- **Found a great bar, club, shop or must-see sight that we don't feature?**

- **Like to tip us off about any information that needs a little updating?**

- **Want to tell us what you love about this handy little guidebook and more importantly how we can make it even handier?**

Then here's your chance to tell all! Send us ideas, discoveries and recommendations today and then look out for your valuable input in the next edition of this title. As an extra 'thank you' from Thomas Cook Publishing, you'll be automatically entered into our exciting monthly prize draw.

Email to the above address (stating the book's title) or write to: CitySpots Project Editor, Thomas Cook Publishing, PO Box 227, Unit 15/16, Coningsby Road, Peterborough PE3 8SB, UK.